EX·LIBRIS

Louis P. Giorgi

Cathedrals

Mervyn Blatch

Cathedrals

BLANDFORD PRESS

Poole   Dorset

7247989

First published in the U.K. 1980
Copyright © 1980 Blandford Press Ltd,
Link House, West Street,
Poole, Dorset, BH15 1LL

British Library Cataloguing in Publication Data

Blatch, Mervyn
    Cathedrals. – (Blandford colour series).
    1. Cathedrals – Europe
    I. Title
    726'.6'094   NA5450

ISBN 0 7137 0943 X (Hardback edition)
ISBN 0 7137 1081 0 X (Paperback edition)

Phototypeset in Monophoto Apollo
by Oliver Burridge and Co. Ltd
Printed in Hong Kong
by South China Printing Co.

Contents

To Gillian, Graham, Timothy and Simon

Acknowledgements

Thanks are due to the many people who have helped with this book, particularly my friend, Alec Clifton-Taylor whose informed and perceptive comments, his journals and especially his book, *The Cathedrals of England*, have been a constant source of inspiration.

Diocesan authorities have been helpful almost without exception, particularly those of Peterborough, Ely and Wells in England and of Bayeux in France.

I have received useful information from a number of Tourist Offices and the assistance of my local library in West Byfleet is greatly appreciated.

The Council for Places of Worship at All Hallows, London Wall, must also be thanked.

Once again, however, it is to my wife that I must express my greatest thanks. She has spent long hours in proof-reading and honing rough patches in the script. The encouragement and help she has given me have been invaluable.

Mr J. Marsden executed the drawings on pages 22, 23, 44 and 131.

Colour photographs have been reproduced by kind permission of the following: Peter Baker—pbp International Picture Library: 30, 35; Philip Baker: 54; M. Blatch: 2, 4, 6, 7, 8, 10, 11, 12, 13, 15, 17, 21, 22, 27, 37, 38, 41, 42, 45, 48, 51, 52; British Tourist Authority: 19; Camera Press Ltd: 24, 39, 50; Miss J. M. Hargreaves: 40; F. L. Harris: 26, 32, 34, 36; C. Hicks, B.Arch., F.R.I.B.A., A.R.P.S.: 14, 16; K. Q. F. Manning: 43; J. N. Merrill: 5; Mrs Rosemary Pardoe: 20; Picturepoint —London: 9, 18; Shell Company of Australia: 53; Miss J. M. Skinner: 33, 46, 47, 55; Swiss National Tourist Office: 44; Dr H. Teed: 29; Van Phillips: 3, 31, 49; Woodmansterne: 1, 25, 28.

Black and white photographs have been reproduced by courtesy of Mr G. Hovenden (page 19); German Embassy (page 116); Netherlands National Tourist Office (page 154); Spanish National Tourist Office (page 148); Swiss National Tourist Office (page 157).

Preface

There are over two thousand residential sees in the Roman Catholic Church, more than three hundred and fifty in the Anglican Communion and the number of Orthodox cathedrals in Russia alone is in excess of fifty although many are no longer used as churches.

In this book, I have attempted to outline the main characteristics of episcopal churches in European countries with brief descriptions of the more important examples architecturally. The variation in style is vast, ranging from the exotic St. Basil's in Moscow to the austere Salisbury in England. Preferences will vary, too, but it would be difficult not to give the palm amongst Gothic cathedrals to the great buildings that arose in France during the thirteenth century.

In mediaeval times, the cathedral was the focal point of activity. Political meetings were held within its walls, the price of grain and livestock discussed; it was the scene of passing-out ceremonies for new guild journeymen and also other less edifying spectacles linked with the Feast of Fools. But, above all, the cathedral to the mediaeval mind was the representative of supernatural reality and its sanctuary was the gateway to Heaven. To echo the words of Jacob after his dream of angels ascending and descending on a ladder: 'How awesome is this place. This is none other than the house of God, and this is the gate of heaven'.

Even today with our more matter-of-fact approach we do not cease to marvel how the mediaeval mason and craftsman with their limited equipment were able to erect such great buildings, exceeding in size all but comparatively recent constructions and still dominating most of the cities in which they are to be found.

1
Belgium

Belgium did not gain independence until 1830 and in its long history has come under many rulers. Architectural influences have therefore flowed into the country from several directions, primarily French and German but also English (St. Michael's Cathedral façade, Brussels), Spanish (later Flamboyant Gothic, e.g. at Antwerp) and Italian (St. Aubain, Namur). When, however, the Flemish people achieved trading prosperity in the fourteenth century, a more local style was developed reflecting 'burgher' opulence and concentrating upon size (e.g. Antwerp, Malines tower) and artistic furnishings rather than mastery of architectural design, harmony of proportion and skill of execution. Lacking the refinement of the best French and English cathedrals it reflects the sober virtues of the market place rather than the spiritual exaltation of high-minded prelates which gave rise to the masterpieces of Chartres, Rheims and Lincoln. And, whilst many of the works of art were of great beauty and excellent craftsmanship, they suffered from both the excesses of the Protestants in a few days of wholesale destruction in August 1566 and the longer lasting depredations of the French Revolutionaries at the end of the eighteenth century who, not content with removing articles of value, demolished whole buildings.

The Romanesque style was largely replaced or overlaid by later construction but Tournai has an outstanding twelfth-century cathedral.

French influence is apparent in the Early Gothic choirs which often took the place of smaller Romanesque ones. This is to be seen in the thirteenth-century examples at Brussels, Ghent, Liège and Tournai which all terminate in an apse, sometimes with ambulatory.

Interiors generally tend to be stereotyped—sober and simple with columns of cylindrical form and acanthus leaf capitals supporting fairly plain arcades. At Brussels and Malines, the columns bear statues of the Apostles symbolising the mediaeval idea of piers and columns bearing the vault of which Christ is the crown. These are also seen in Germany and other countries. Tall clerestories are a feature but traceried rose-windows are rare.

The art of making stained glass attained its peak in the twelfth/thirteenth centuries but there is none in the cathedrals of this date. Most of what is to be seen is sixteenth-century or later, being historical in content rather than symbolic or biblical.

Despite the fearful toll of mediaeval works of art taken by Protestant iconoclasm and Revolutionary fanaticism, others have been found, particularly paintings, altarpieces and screens. They tend, however, to distract one from the architecture. The pulpits are not likely to be overlooked, as these eighteenth-century furnishings are carved into unbelievable shapes and are excessively ornate with a riot of decoration typical of Baroque and Rococo styles. They are usually found on the south side of the nave.

Belgium had a much greater choice of materials than the Netherlands (which is almost entirely devoid of good building stone). Although brick is found in the tower, columns and in-filling of vaults at Bruges, in the exterior of Namur and in the nave of Ghent, combined with stone, Belgium could draw on fine-grained bluish-grey Tournai limestone, Lède sandstone and various other materials such as dark brown ironstone, the slate and light yellow-coloured stones of Liège and marble from the Ardennes.

The following are brief descriptions of Belgium's cathedrals.

Antwerp. The cathedral of Antwerp, begun in 1352 and not completed until 1584, occupies nearly a hectare of ground and is the largest church in Belgium. With three aisles on each side, the nave is unusually wide but, although harmonious in style, it lacks warmth; the one hundred and twenty-five pillars which support it are without capitals so that the arches flow into them without interruption.

The north tower and spire, which reach a height of 122 m (400 ft), were completed in 1521 in Flamboyant Gothic style. They bear a family resemblance to the earlier tower and spire of the Town Hall in the Grand-Place of Brussels. A landmark for miles around, it has been described as 'straight as a cry, beautiful as a mast, clear as a candle'. Certainly its lace-work effect is very handsome.

The cathedral possesses four examples of the work of the great Flemish painter, Peter Paul Rubens, including the world-famous *Descent from the Cross* in the south transept.

Bruges. The brick Cathedral of St. Saviour took the place of St. Donation, destroyed by the Revolutionaries, as the episcopal church when the see was recreated in 1834. After severe damage by fire in 1358, the nave and transepts were immediately rebuilt but the ambulatory and choir chapels were not completed until 1530. The choir, which is the oldest part, goes back to the thirteenth/fourteenth century. The exterior is disfigured by a neo-Romanesque top stage, added to the tower between 1844 and 1871, and is generally plain with large windows.

The well-proportioned interior has good stalls dating from 1478 with finely carved armrests and lively misericords; they are decorated with the coats of arms of the Knights of the Golden Fleece; there are also extensive tapestries. The Baroque rood-screen in bronze, wood and marble dates from 1679–82 and surmounts yellow brass doors of 1708.

Brussels. The Collegiate Church of St. Michael (popularly known as St. Gudule) is the spiritual centre of Brussels. It has suffered much over the years from vandalism and in 1789 it was suggested that the church should be pulled down and turned into a theatre. Construction lasted from 1220 to the end of the fifteenth century; the choir, transepts, nave, arcades and south aisle were completed in 1273, the latest work, apart from the chapels, being the unfinished western towers, 69 m (226 ft) high. There was a restoration in 1848–56.

The western façade is the most striking example of English influence and has been likened to that of Westminster Abbey.

In the Chapel of the Holy Sacrament on the north side (built in 1534–39) some of Belgium's best glass is to be seen; many of the characters and scenes associated with the cathedral's history are depicted. In the Maes Chapel in the apse (rebuilt in Baroque style between 1666 and 1678 and crowned by a cupola with skylight) there is a charming bust of the Virgin and Child and there are some good monuments in the Chapel of the Blessed Sacrament (1649–53).

Ghent. St. Bavo's was the scene in 1500 of the baptism of the Emperor Charles V and received generous contributions from him later for the building of the nave. It became a cathedral in 1559.

Earlier the chancel had been built in Flamboyant Gothic style in the first half of the fourteenth century and the 82 m (269 ft) high tower was started in the middle of the fifteenth century. Due to the religious wars, this was not completed until a hundred years later in 1554. By this time, work had begun on the nave and transepts linking the tower with the chancel. The sixteenth-century nave is only four bays long owing to the earlier building of the tower. Skilful use of materials, however, (white Lède sandstone for the piers and vaulting ribs, and brick for the walls and vault infilling creates a harmonious transition to the much earlier raised chancel of greyish-blue Tournai limestone. The ribs are arranged in a network pattern.

Part of the old Romanesque crypt remains in the present one which extends the whole length and breadth of the chancel.

Prominent amongst many furnishings and fittings of note is the polyptych called *The Mystic Lamb* in the sixth chapel of the south choir ambulatory. This great work, ascribed to one or both of the van Eyck brothers, took twelve years to complete (1420–32) and has been called the greatest work of art in Belgium. Only the four panels in the central portion, however, are original, the remainder being copies. There are no less than two hundred and forty-eight figures in its composition. There is also a painting by Rubens (*The Conversion of St. Bavo*) and a retable by Janssens (*Jesus in the Midst of the Doctors*). The pulpit, dating from 1745, is an extraordinary mixture of marble and oak.

Liège. As at Bruges, the present cathedral (St. Paul's) replaced an earlier one (St. Lambert's) demolished at the time of the French Revolution. In the past, the bishops of Liège had great power and were in fact prince-bishops. The building was mainly erected between 1232 and 1289 and is therefore in Early Gothic style. In 1334, the original flat east end was replaced by a polygonal apse. There was much restoration and alteration in the middle of the nineteenth century and repairs had to be made after the War owing to damage caused by a flying bomb in 1945.

The exterior is made sombre by the dark colour of the stone and the main feature is the western tower, which, however, was only completed with spire and four bell-turrets in 1811. Internally, the vista to the tall windows of the apse with notable mid-sixteenth-century glass is impressive. The vaults were decorated at the same time with poly-chromed scroll patterns.

Amongst furnishings and treasures must be mentioned the outstanding stained glass window of 1530 in the south transept depicting the Coronation of the Virgin, the stalls (the finest in Belgian cathedrals), the reliquary of St. Lambert containing his skull (his body is preserved in a shrine of 1896 displayed in the church) and the pulpit of 1844. The treasury in which the St. Lambert reliquary is kept is entered from the eastern walk of the cloisters on the south side.

Malines. The archi-episcopal cathedral of St. Rombaut is memorable for its huge western tower, started in 1452 and planned to have a spire of 168 m (550 ft). As happened so often, it was never completed, work stopping in 1546. Nevertheless, with its strong vertical emphasis, forceful and yet light, it makes a powerful impression which caused Vauban, the famous military engineer of Louis XIV of France, to call it the eighth wonder of the world.

The harmonious interior consists of thirteenth-century nave/transepts and a fourteenth-century choir, dominated by an immense Baroque altarpiece surmounted by a statue of St. Rombaut.

The pulpit is a supreme example of the tendency to carve in fantastic forms and to splash on decoration without regard to the surroundings. The theme is the Conversion of St. Paul; there is a mass of rock at the base and the handrail is carved in the form of a fallen tree whilst dotted around are small creatures.

In the south transept is a poignant *Crucifixion* by Van Dyck.

Malmédy. The Cathedral of St. Peter, St. Paul and St. Quirin at Malmédy is an abbey church erected between 1776 and 1784 in Baroque style. It is crowned by a large dome culminating in a lantern-turret at the crossing. Interesting furnishings include pulpit, Louis XIV font and Louis XVI stalls.

Namur. St. Aubain's at Namur is Belgium's only Baroque cathedral, built between 1751 and 1767 by an Italian architect.

Of excellent proportions, the building is distinguished by the central dome and the consistency of its design.

Tournai. This is the outstanding cathedral of Belgium and basically Romanesque. With its multiplicity of towers—there were once two more flanking the eastern part—and its apsidal transepts, the original Romanesque building was clearly derived from the mid-Rhenish style of Maria Laach (abbey), Speyer and Worms in Germany. The five towers are all of the same height 83 m (272 ft) but the one over the crossing is broader and has a lantern with four little pyramids at the corners; the tower next to the nave on the north side was once used as a prison.

The twelfth-century nave has lively capitals in the style of the time but the ordonnance of four storeys is marred by the second or tribune stage being of the same height as the main arcade; the columns have no bases and the arches are square-edged without chamfers or mouldings. The upper part is plastered in white making a shrill contrast with the bluish-grey limestone below.

A screen of polychrome marble separates the nave from the Gothic choir of 1242, which is almost as long as the nave; it is richly carved and skilfully executed but it is questionable whether this Renaissance furnishing—by the Flemish artist Cornelis de Vriendt and dating from 1572—apart from closing the vista, is in tune with the lightness of the choir and the robust austerity of the nave.

The fine treasury contains two richly executed thirteenth-century reliquaries and the chasuble of Thomas à Becket, who was in Tournai in 1170, the year he was murdered.

For five years from 1513 to 1518, Tournai was under English domination and during this period the see was occupied by Cardinal Wolsey.

2
British Isles

Although at least three English bishops attended the Council of Arles in 314, the story of cathedrals in the British Isles does not begin until the foundation in the year 601 of St. Paul's Cathedral in London by Bishop Mellitus at the request of King Ethelbert. During the Saxon period there were fine cathedrals at Canterbury, Durham, Winchester and Worcester but all that is left above ground of Saxon diocesan churches are a few rubbly remains at North Elmham—a remote place in Norfolk, the crypt at Ripon and re-used baluster shafts in the triforium of the south transept at St. Albans.

In pre-Conquest times the establishment of a see depended upon the goodwill of the local ruler so that the boundaries of the diocese tended to coincide with those of the secular power but, under the centralised rule of the Norman kings, sees were transferred from smaller places to the principal towns in each diocese. Crediton had already been replaced by Exeter in 1050 before the Conquest but after 1066 the process was accelerated and the see of Dorchester was moved to Lincoln, Sherborne to Salisbury, Selsey to Chichester, Lichfield to Chester and later to Coventry, and North Elmham to Norwich *via* Thetford.

At the same time, a massive programme of rebuilding was undertaken and the Normans, who were enthusiastic builders, lost no time in pulling down many of the Saxon churches and replacing them with new buildings of their own design. Of the seventeen cathedrals existing at the time of the Reformation in the sixteenth century, only Lichfield, Salisbury and Wells are entirely Gothic.

Already we can see a divergence from the development of French cathedral architecture in the many examples of fine diocesan churches in the British Isles from the Norman period whereas the major surviving buildings in France of that era are abbeys. This underlines the importance in the Norman hierarchy of bishops, who were given considerable powers by William the Conqueror, who, despite papal warnings, retained overall supremacy of the English Church. The Bishop of Durham's powers were, in fact, akin to those of the prince-bishops of Austria, Belgium and Germany. Entrusted with the guardianship of the land and of the shrine of St. Cuthbert in an exposed area near the Scottish border, the bishop acted in lieu of the king. In Anglo-Saxon times, Durham had been a community of monks under a bishop and this arrangement, peculiar to England, was followed elsewhere in this country. The bishop was the titular abbot but the effective head of the monastic establishment was the prior. Eight of the seventeen mediaeval English cathedrals were of this so-called cathedral-priory type (Canterbury, Carlisle, Durham, Ely, Norwich, Rochester, Winchester and Worcester). It was not a particularly happy arrangement and led to constant friction between bishop and prior as to their respective rights.

Apart from the organisational aspects, important architectural effects flowed from this combining of episcopal and monastic buildings for, in order to accommodate the lay congregations and to leave the choir free for the daily offices, very long naves were required and therefore many of the English cathedrals emphasise length rather than width or height.

The remaining diocesan churches were served by either Canons Regular or Secular Canons. The episcopal seats of this type, known since the reign of Henry VIII as Cathedrals of the Old Foundation, are Chichester, Exeter, Hereford, Lichfield, Lincoln, London, Salisbury, York and Wells.

Norman. The earliest Norman work, dating from the time of William the Conqueror, is to be seen at St. Albans and Winchester. Prior to the Reformation, St. Albans—made a cathedral in 1877—was the premier abbey in the country. Despite a punitive nineteenth-century restoration, the north transept gives a good idea of the uncompromising and rugged appearance of early Norman but the transepts at Winchester, built between 1079 and 1093 of Isle of Wight limestone, are more impressive.

The development of this style, which plays such an important part in English cathedral architecture, will be followed in the individual descriptions of the churches.

Early English. In 1174, a disaster struck the monks of Canterbury when a fire spread from the town to the roof of the cathedral, destroying much of the eastern part of the building. The distracted monks eventually decided to call in a Frenchman, William of Sens, to set about the reconstruction and he was in touch with the new developments at St. Denis in Paris, using pointed arches and rib vaults. This heralded the great Gothic revolution.

The style, which came to be known in the British Isles as Early English, was next employed at Wells and the work there may have begun at the same time as William of Sens was busy at Canterbury but to a completely different design. This was followed by Lincoln for the very curious reason that the old Romanesque cathedral suffered an earthquake tremor in 1185, so severe that, except for the west front, the whole building had to be taken down. Meanwhile, another opportunity occurred to build anew in the Gothic style in the south. Because of various circumstances, chiefly the lack of water, authority was given to the bishop to transfer his see from Old Sarum on a cold exposed position outside Salisbury to the town itself. Other cathedrals to show Early English work are Carlisle (choir), Chester (chapter-house), Durham (Chapel of the Nine Altars), Ely (presbytery), Southwark (choir and retro-choir), Worcester (choir, eastern transepts and retro-choir) and York (transepts).

Decorated. Towards the close of the thirteenth century, the ascetic force in England declined and architecture became more human. There was less emphasis on height and more on breadth so that churches became less austere. It was the age of chivalry and a time when women were held in high esteem, reflected in the veneration accorded to the Virgin Mary and the addition of Lady Chapels to many cathedrals. Tracery developed in windows, first Geometrical then Reticulated and finally Flowing and Intricate. Arches continued to be pointed but less sharply. Decoration became richer. At about the same time, and perhaps another facet of the same spirit, cloisters were added to some of the non-monastic cathedrals merely because they were pleasant areas in which to stroll.

Contrary to what was happening in France, the first half of the fourteenth century in England was a time of relative prosperity but with the fear of movable possessions being requisitioned to provide money for the war against France, the church authorities applied more of their wealth to structural improvements rather than to furnishings.

The outstanding example of this so-called Decorated style which lasted roughly over the reigns of the first three Edwards (1272 to 1377), is Exeter which is the most consistent in design of English mediaeval cathedrals with the exception of Salisbury.

Perpendicular. Before the end of the Decorated phase, a new style of wholly English Gothic architecture developed in the West Country, where an advanced school of Severn masons were experimenting. The opportunity to use it on a large scale occurred when the body of the English king, Edward II, who had been brutally murdered at Berkeley Castle in Gloucestershire was secured by the Abbot of Gloucester Abbey (later the Cathedral) who built a shrine for him. This attracted large numbers of pilgrims whose offerings provided the Abbot with sufficient funds to embark upon a major rebuilding programme which took about one hundred and fifty years to complete.

Except for the Norman nave the whole of the Abbey was either refashioned or rebuilt in the new style which came to be known as Perpendicular although, as horizontal transoms were frequently used in windows and panelling, it might be more appropriate to call it Rectilinear. There was, however, emphasis on the upward line. Mullions were carried up to the head of the window, arches tended to be more obtuse and often four-centred—in Tudor times, even straight-headed. Greater importance was given to interiors than to exteriors and the aim was to produce a large hall lit by large windows giving a glass-house effect. This age, however, also contributed glorious towers.

The major works of the Perpendicular period in cathedrals are the naves of Canterbury and Winchester, and the choir of York. Of towers, the most notable are Worcester, Gloucester and especially Canterbury's central 'Bell Harry'—the finest in the British Isles. At Wells, the western towers were added to the façade and the central tower raised and given a splendid, much-pinnacled crown. Although no longer considered essential in this more secular age, new spires were added to Norwich and Chichester.

An outstanding achievement of the architects of the Perpendicular period was the skill they attained in constructing beautiful vaults. At Norwich, the cathedral was completely revaulted towards the end of the fifteenth century and the new naves at Canterbury and Winchester also received fine lierne examples. An English invention was the fanvault in which half cones were used, most familiarly in the cloisters of Gloucester (one of the earliest) but also in the retro-choir of Peterborough and charmingly in Canterbury's 'Bell Harry'. The final culmination of virtuosity in this field is to be seen in the choir of Oxford Cathedral where, towards the end of the fifteenth century, a lierne vault was built with pendant lanterns.

Post-Reformation. After the Reformation, English cathedrals suffered greatly, first from the hazards of the Civil War and later from neglect. The only new diocesan edifice to be built during the three hundred years between the end of the mediaeval age (mid-sixteenth century) and the beginning of the Victorian period (1837) was Wren's St. Paul's in London which replaced Old St. Paul's, irreparably damaged in the Great Fire of 1666.

With emancipation in 1829, Roman Catholics were in a position to build cathedrals for their worship and the outstanding examples architecturally are Westminster in London and the modern ones at Liverpool and Bristol.

The Anglican Church created many additional sees in the nineteenth century including Truro where a new cathedral was built but in most cases parish churches were elevated to episcopal status.

In the present century new mother churches have been built in Coventry, Guildford and Liverpool.

Of England's forty-two cathedrals, there are four which stand out architecturally—Canterbury, Durham, Lincoln and Wells—and these are described in some detail before surveying the remainder regionally.

Canterbury. Like many English diocesan churches this building is a mixture of styles with a Norman crypt, an early Gothic choir and a magnificent Perpendicular nave.

The Norman crypt was completed by 1107 and is famed for the carving of the capitals carried out shortly afterwards. Fabulous creatures are depicted in a most lively manner.

Rebuilding of the choir in Gothic style (after the disastrous fire) took place between 1175 and 1185 and was therefore in advance of Peterborough which was still being built in the Norman style by the end of the twelfth century. The length was extended to house the shrine of Thomas à Becket and, until the Reformation, this shrine in the corona (so called because of the crown of Becket's head being sliced off during his murder in 1170) became the leading goal of pilgrimage in England, bringing great riches to the cathedral. The round columns of the choir with Corinthian capitals are similar to those of Laon, Lisieux and Notre-Dame de Paris in France.

The glory, however, of the eastern part of Canterbury is its late twelfth/thirteenth-century stained glass which, although only in part surviving, is—with its vivid ruby, blue, green and other colours—the finest in England.

The early Perpendicular nave, built between 1378 and 1405 by a famous master-mason, Henry Yevele, who did much work at Westminster, is a noble light creation with an attractive lierne vault.

The mediaeval work culminates in the majestic central tower. With its strong vertical emphasis and beautiful pinnacles this tower, erected between 1494 and 1497, faced with Caen stone but brick within, is affectionately known as 'Bell Harry'.

Durham. Cathedral and university are perched above the town on a rock encircled by a horseshoe bend of the River Wear. Except for the east end most of the three towers and the cloisters, the cathedral is en-

Sanctuary doorknocker of Romanesque metalwork, Durham, British Isles.

tirely Norman in design. Proud symbol of a powerful bishop, this mighty building is universally regarded as the outstanding Romanesque church in Europe and certainly deserves its place amongst the first four of any style in England. The huge nave piers are alternately circular and compound (i.e. with engaged shafts) and are incised with various motifs (diaper, chevron, fluted; in the choir and transepts, spiral is used). The transepts are noted for having the earliest high-level ribbed vaults in

Europe, dating from about 1110 and the nave, vaulted later, made the first great breakthrough to the Gothic ribbed vaults by having the transverse arches pointed, thus enabling the ridge rib to be level.

Towards the end of the period of Norman architecture the large Galilee Porch (1170–75) with its exuberant decoration of chevrons, etc. was added, thus providing a Lady Chapel in the most unusual position of the west end.

If the west end at Durham is out of the ordinary so also is the east end, for the Chapel of the Nine Altars, erected between 1242 and about 1280, stretches out on the north and south sides to form another pair of transepts, a peculiarly northern arrangement not found elsewhere in England.

The heightening of the central tower was the result of the old one being struck by lightning in 1429. It was raised in two stages to a height of 66 m (218 ft), a not altogether successful design, but giving it the necessary altitude in relation to the two western towers.

One should seek out the bronze 'Sanctuary' knocker, normally on the north-west door, an outstanding example of Romanesque metal-work with marvellously stylised hair.

Lincoln. Whilst not without its faults, notably the lowness of the nave and the somewhat unsatisfactory proportions, this cathedral is nevertheless one of the loveliest products of the Early English and Decorated styles of architecture and, Durham apart, the most dramatically sited.

After the 1185 earthquake tremor, the opportunity was taken to construct a new cathedral, the design drawn up at the beginning of 1192 being followed through until completion in 1280, although there remained to be built the upper parts of the three towers and the cloisters. Purbeck marble (not a true marble but a limestone which will take a polish) was used to a greater degree than in any other English church, its varying colours contrasting with the honey-coloured oolitic limestone which was the main building material. Around the Norman part of the great façade which survived, the wide high Gothic screen was constructed with its mass of arcading, impressive but failing to articulate with the main structure.

The Decorated work consists of the delightful Angel Choir (1256–80), which received its name from the thirty angels in the spandrels of the upper arcade; the large east window is striking with its Geometrical tracery but the richness of the decoration and the open tracery of the clerestory are outstanding.

Perhaps, however, the greatest pleasures of the interior of Lincoln are the stone doorways leading from the transepts to the choir aisles, masterpieces of carving still today wonderfully crisp. They date from the same time as the Angel Choir.

By 1300 the main structure was complete but early in the fourteenth century the sumptuous pulpitum or choir screen was added with very rich ornamentation and the end wall of the south transept reconstructed with a new rose-window—the famous *Bishop's Eye*—with quite outstanding tracery and filled with mediaeval glass fragments. At the same time, the central tower was heightened and a new spire added (this was destroyed during a storm in 1548). The two western towers were raised later. The combination of these three noble towers is yet another of the glories of this magnificent cathedral.

Wells. At about the same time as the choir of Canterbury was being rebuilt in the second half of the twelfth century, work started on a cathedral at Wells in Somerset, but to a design completely different from that of Canterbury. There is no French influence but we see at Wells the first mediaeval mother church in England with pointed arches throughout. Transepts, nave, north porch and most of the great west front except for the towers (not added until two hundred years later) were completed by about 1240. Although the nave is small and only 20 m (67 ft) high, the beautifully clustered piers and the admirable proportions make it a source of great pleasure, despite the incongruous scissor-arches inserted at the east end to help support the central tower. Added enjoyment is afforded by the capitals of the nave and transept piers with delightful genre scenes—notably the fruit-stealers and the man with toothache—and perhaps best of all the lizard.

The west front, designed as a screen for the display of statues to illustrate the triumph of the Church, still retains about half of its original three hundred and forty figures and is the finest and, except for Peterborough, the widest example in England. The design is singularly harmonious, with its strong horizontal emphasis balanced by the vertical punctuation of the buttresses and the low unpinnacled towers which are admirably adapted to the overall scheme.

The late thirteenth to mid fourteenth century saw notable additions. An elevated chapter-house was built on the north side reached by a stairway which divides at the top to lead to the bridge across the road to the Vicars' Close, thus giving the exquisite branching effect. The beautiful chapter-house is enriched with heads on the canopies of the fifty-one stalls and some original glass in the tracery lights of the windows, but the most spectacular feature is the vault with thirty-two ribs rising from the central shaft and resembling a palm tree.

The presbytery and Lady Chapel with retro-choir between afford charming vistas and display some elaborate vaulting including early examples of lierne type. These retain much mediaeval stained glass.

Finally, the seal was placed on this enchanting building by erecting the 38 m (125 ft) western towers and later raising the central tower to a height of 55 m (182 ft) giving it a much-pinnacled crown. The view from the south-east shows how beautiful a composition this makes.

Carved capital depicting man with tooth-ache, Wells, British Isles.

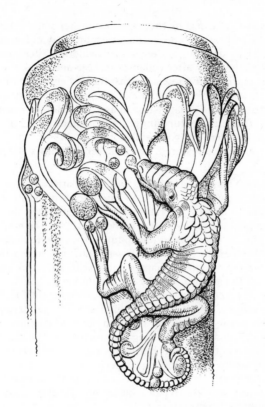

Carved capital depicting lizard, Wells, British Isles.

NORTH ENGLAND (Carlisle, Durham, Liverpool, Ripon, York)

This area contains a mixed group of very large (Durham—see separate description—and York) and small cathedrals (Carlisle, Ripon), plus two twentieth century creations at Liverpool (see Chapter 9).

Carlisle. Only a truncated portion of its former state, due to the destruction of all but two bays of the nave by the Scots in about 1650, its beauty is concentrated on the eastern end and especially on its nine-light Decorated window 15 m (51 ft) high, one of the loveliest in England.

Ripon. Made a cathedral in 1836, this is a rather squat building with good western and eastern ends—the former an essay in lancets and the latter with a fine seven-light Geometrical window. There were partial rebuildings of the choir after collapses in 1288 and 1458, the latter including part of the central tower, so that the east end combines work of three periods and has both round and pointed arches. The crossing is an ill-assorted mixture of late Norman and Perpendicular work.

The large fifteenth-century pulpitum completely cuts off the nave from the choir. There are good stalls of about 1490 with a fine set of misericords but much restored, and fourteenth-century sedilia.

York. Although a majestic building with many attractive features, and possessing more mediaeval glass than any other British cathedral, York somehow fails to impress overall except by its size (it is the largest of England's mediaeval cathedrals). The best parts are the east end with one of the biggest windows in the country, the austere north transept with its noble five lancets (the *Five Sisters*), each measuring 16 m (53 ft) in height, and the octagonal chapter-house with attractive star-shaped vault and fine Geometrical tracery in the windows.

The nave was erected between 1291 and the end of the first half of the fourteenth century. Despite being the highest in the country after Westminster Abbey, the wide spaces between the piers diminish the effect and the use of wood in the vaulting is unfortunate. The chapter-house and west front—notable for its buttresses and splendid central window with exceptionally fine Flowing tracery—were completed in 1345 whilst the Perpendicular towers were added in the fifteenth century, the richly decorated western pair contrasting with the massive sobriety of the unpinnacled central tower.

EAST ENGLAND (Ely, Lincoln, Norwich, Peterborough, Southwell)

This group embraces some of the finest Norman work, all except Lincoln (see separate description) having Norman naves.

Ely. The single western tower—unique in English cathedrals—and octagon give the church a striking individuality and sited as it is in very low-lying country the building is a landmark for miles around. The tower forms part of the west front which once consisted of a complete pair of transepts but unfortunately the north-western one collapsed in the fifteenth century. Even in its truncated form, however, this is the finest Norman façade in the country with its rich and varied decoration of blind arcading.

It is late Norman work but the nave of twelve bays—long even for England—is early. Bare of ornament, its austerity contrasts strikingly with the beauty of the mature Early English presbytery; the cambered ceiling is of wood. The presbytery (1234–52) took the place of, and is considerably longer than, the old apsed Norman choir. Purbeck marble, dogtooth decoration on the mouldings, vaulting and bosses are used to great advantage and the design is full of appeal.

In 1322, the central tower—as happened so often with Norman towers —fell, providing the opportunity to erect a most ingenious structure to cover the central space. Although the lantern is of wood, the surrounding octagon is stone and together they afford one of the most exciting experiences in English architecture as one looks up at the beautiful vault and the lantern beyond with its eight-pointed star roof. At the same time, the Lady Chapel was added—the largest in England with the widest mediaeval vault (a span of 14 m [46 ft]).

Only the richly sculptured Norman doorways, formerly providing access, remain of the cloisters. The pair of corbel heads supporting the lintel of the Prior's Door with their bulging eyes are full of life.

Norwich. Even longer than the nave at Ely is the Norman one at Norwich but whereas the former, and also the later example at Peterborough, have wooden ceilings, the whole of the nave, presbytery and transepts of Norwich received gracious lierne stone vaults in the second half of the fifteenth/beginning of the sixteenth century. Prior to this, and following the fall of the original wooden spire in a gale in 1362, the eastern end was provided with a much taller clerestory having lofty traceried windows, and the combination of extra height with the lierne vault creates a delightful ensemble. Particularly fine is the apse with ambulatory and tribune both carried round in a semicircle, a unique arrangement in English cathedrals, creating a three-dimensional effect and providing externally, with the flying buttresses to support the vault, a welcome variant to the usual flat east end.

The spire, rebuilt after the wooden one had been blown down, was struck by lightning a century later and the present spire, at 96 m (315 ft) the second tallest in England, was built in the latter part of the fifteenth century. Together with the well-proportioned Norman tower, this graceful addition helps to create a noble steeple with a distinctive silhouette.

The large two-storeyed cloisters took from 1297 to about 1430 to build but the design remained consistent and is enlivened with nearly four hundred re-coloured bosses. Leading into them in the north-east corner is a charming portal in the Decorated style of about 1310 with seven small figures in the arch arranged radially and having gables, alternately ogee-shaped, behind them.

Peterborough. More consistently Norman than Ely, this has an un-interrupted vista from west to east. Being later in date, it is more richly ornamented and the cambered nave ceiling dating from about 1220, decorated with lozenge patterns, still retains its original colouring.

There is, however, notable post-Norman work at each end ranging from the early Gothic western front with three deeply recessed and lofty moulded arches (25 m [81 ft] high) to the late Gothic retro-choir, extending the whole width of the church beyond the central apse with its beautiful fan-vaulting and enriched by decorative panelling below the windows. It was begun about 1500.

At the eastern end of the cathedral there is a notable Anglo-Saxon piece of sculpture thought to be a shrine and dated as probably about 800 with a pitched roof and carved figures on the sides. It is called the Hedda Stone although Abbot Hedda was murdered by the Danes many years later.

Peterborough also possesses a rare mediaeval wooden tread-wheel for lifting stones.

Southwell. A smallish cathedral in the smallest of cities, Southwell in Nottinghamshire, not raised to diocesan rank until 1884, has much to offer the visitor.

Despite its somewhat flat elevations, the exterior is made interesting by its west front, the low central tower and the unusual porthole clerestory windows.

The interior is a mixture of Norman nave with short, massive cylin-drical columns and attractive Early English chancel, separated by a notable pulpitum richly ornamented in the Decorated style and dating from about 1350.

But the glory of Southwell and the respect in which it is supreme is the carving of the leaves on the capitals and canopies above the canons' stalls of the thirteenth-century chapter-house, the vestibule leading to it and on the splendid entrance portal. They are drawn in glorious pro-fusion from nature but carefully adapted to the architectural require-ments. The depth of the undercutting and the resultant shadows make these a triumph of the stone carver's art and have earned justifiable renown as the *Leaves of Southwell*.

SOUTH-EAST ENGLAND (Canterbury, Chichester, Guildford, London [St. Paul's and Southwark], St. Albans)

This group ranges from the oldest to the newest—from the early Norman of St. Albans, to the largely post-War but traditional Cathedral of Guildford (see Chapter 9), including some of the most famous (Canterbury—see separate description—and St. Paul's) and others more modest.

Chichester. This is the only mediaeval cathedral in England visible from the sea. The style is mainly Norman but perhaps the most important part architecturally is the transitional Gothic retro-choir and the Decorated three eastern bays of the long Lady Chapel. Although small, this church has a double-aisled nave which is the widest, except for that at York, of any English cathedral. In 1861, the spire over the central tower quietly subsided into the body of the church but has been rebuilt, faithfully following the old model.

Chichester is unique for its detached belfry on the south-west corner and chiefly memorable for its two Romanesque sculptures on the south wall of the choir aisle depicting *Christ coming to the House of Mary of Bethany* and the *Raising of Lazarus*. The sorrow on the face of Christ in the former is intensely moving and these two pieces of carving are among the finest Norman sculpture in the country.

London (St. Paul's). After Canterbury, this is by far the most important of the group architecturally. Following the Great Fire of London in 1666, it was decided to rebuild Old St. Paul's, and Wren designed and completed the new cathedral in his own lifetime in a mixture of Classical and Baroque styles. The plan follows the Classical standards of proportion and is symmetrical throughout. Wren, although never having visited the city, drew heavily on Rome. The result, except for the space under the dome, is an interior somewhat lacking in warmth but the furnishings and sculpture, carried out by a team of brilliant craftsmen—and indeed the architecture itself—give much to enjoy. Wren engaged Grinling Gibbons to make the fine stalls and screen behind, as well as most of the organ-case, and the French smith, Jean Tijou, to execute the iron-work which includes some splendid wrought-iron gates and screens. Recent cleaning has revealed much delightful stone carving with an abundance of cherubs' heads, swags and drops of fruit and flowers still in excellent condition due to the quality of the Portland stone used. Some of the stonework was carried out by Grinling Gibbons. The sculpture is seen to best advantage over the Dean's Door in the south-west corner carved by John Thompson.

But the glory of St. Paul's is the dome, generally regarded as supreme in the world, in which Wren showed his most brilliant inventiveness. It consists of two main sections, a brick cone supporting the lovely lantern at the top from which spreads, like an umbrella, the outer dome of wood, sheathed in lead, the whole rising to a height of 111 m (364 ft). The west towers, the most Baroque part of the building, are also notable examples of Wren's virtuosity, constructed towards the end of the work and designed by him when he was seventy-five years old.

London (Southwark). Once the Augustinian priory church of St. Mary Overie, and, after the Reformation, the parish church, it was elevated to cathedral status in 1905. The nave, which had fallen into decay, was twice rebuilt in the nineteenth century, the present one dating from 1890–97. The very cramped site was reduced in 1830 by the demolition of the Lady Chapel for road-widening but the Early English choir separated from the retro-choir by a very lofty but much restored reredos, dating from about 1520 with renewed statues, remains. This eastern limb is full of pleasures, especially the four chapels of the retro-choir, well-vaulted and separated from one another by attractive screens. Much refacing as a result of London grime has been necessary but the pinnacled central tower with chequer-work decoration on the parapet remains a commanding feature of the river skyline.

There are many fine furnishings and monuments, notably the magnificent chandelier given to the church in 1680; the crown, mitre and dove symbolise the concern of the age for the relationship between Church and State.

St. Albans. With its immensely long nave, the cathedral is greatly marred by a particularly insensitive nineteenth-century restoration but the transepts are telling examples of Norman architecture from the time of William the Conqueror.

Externally, the main feature is the tower largely built of Roman bricks. Internally, the most interesting parts are the crossing, the thirteenth/fourteenth-century wall paintings on the nave piers, the fifteenth-century panels of the choir ceiling and the stone rood-screen (the only one in an English cathedral) of about 1380. Many of the paintings are on the west face of the piers which indicates that they were used as reredoses to some of the many altars needed in a mediaeval church. St. Albans also has a fine reredos of 1484 with canopied niches (but with Victorian statues) and a unique fifteenth-century feretory or watching chamber from which guard was kept on the shrine of St. Alban, England's first martyr.

SOUTH/SOUTH-WEST ENGLAND (Exeter, Salisbury, Wells, Winchester)

This group comprises two of the most consistent in design of England's mediaeval cathedrals (Exeter, Salisbury), perhaps the most gracious (Wells—see separate description), and one which is a blend of the earliest and latest mediaeval styles (Winchester).

Exeter. This cathedral has the longest unbroken roof in England but the lack of height due to the limitations imposed by the retention of the unusually sited transeptal Norman towers, and perhaps also the incorporation of part of the old Norman walls, makes for an unimpressive exterior. The western screen, dating from about 1346–1375, is more like a reredos and, although the informal but much weathered statues are largely original, it fails to articulate with the main building and blocks the lower half of the west window.

But these imperfections are forgotten as one enters, for we see here the finest and longest (91 m [300 ft]) vault in England, made possible by the absence of a central tower. It is of the tierceron type in which additional ribs are inserted between the springing points and the ridge. The nave and choir, together with the charming intervening pulpitum (1318–25), were erected between 1275 and 1369 and are the most beautiful expression of the Decorated style, which these dates approximately span, to be seen in the country, made even more enjoyable by the varieties of stone used. Richly shafted piers of unpolished Purbeck limestone, finely moulded arches, a profusion of bosses, numerous delightful corbels mainly of sandstone, create one great architectural vista far removed from the austerity of Early English to be seen at Salisbury. The only criticisms are the lack of height (only 21 m [69 ft]) in relation to width and the obtrusiveness of the organ.

One must single out the Bishop's Throne (1313–17), considered by Pevsner as 'the most exquisite piece of woodwork of its date in England and perhaps in Europe', the elaborately ornamented sedilia of about 1320 and the set of nearly fifty misericords dating from 1260–80 and therefore the earliest in England (except for isolated examples at Christchurch Priory, Dorset, and at Westminster, London).

Exeter cathedral was struck by bombs in May 1942 but the damage has been made good.

Salisbury. Work on the cathedral began in 1220 and in the comparatively short period of forty-five years the main structure was erected in one style—the purest Early English. The cloisters and chapter-house were added and completed by 1284 but it was not until 1334 that a start was made on the tower and spire. This superb creation—the highest (123 m [404 ft]) and the most beautiful in England—was completed about 1380 in the Decorated style. So perfect is the design that its undue size in relation to the rest of the building is overlooked. In fact, the general picture from the entrance to the close—a happy eighteenth-century addition and the best example of this very English feature—is a delight.

Closer inspection is less satisfying. The lack of external decoration and the poor west front detract from one's pleasure and, although the proportions of the interior and the clarity of the plan are a great asset, the plainness of the decoration, the absence of sculpture and the rather strident contrast between the grey limestone and the varnished black Purbeck marble shafts, together with the loss of the old glass, create a coldness and lack of mystery about the interior which is disturbing. It is not helped by the meagre quantity of mediaeval furnishings, although there is a huge brass in the north-east transept to Bishop Wyville, who died in 1375, and the oldest English military effigy (William Longespée —1226).

The splendid cloisters, the largest in England, are on a lavish scale with their traceried arcades enclosing a garth with two spreading cedar trees.

Winchester. As one rounds the corner of the road leading into the city from Alresford, the low-lying cathedral with its squat Norman central tower and massive bulk lies before the visitor. Size and strength are the dominant impressions—a reminder of the Norman Conqueror in whose reign the robust and severely plain north and south transepts of his new cathedral were built. In general, however, Winchester with its weak western façade is less impressive externally than within.

As at Exeter, one is unprepared for the majesty of the interior. At about the same time (second half of the fourteenth century) as Henry Yevele rebuilt the nave at Canterbury, work was undertaken at Winchester but whereas Yevele took down the nave at Canterbury and started again, William Wynford at Winchester left the old Norman nave and encased it with a new design in the Perpendicular style. There are many differences of detail, the main impression being that Winchester is longer and darker whilst Canterbury is more spacious and lighter with a lofty arcade and tall aisles; the Canterbury piers are slender and vertical lines are emphasised. At Winchester, there is a solemn grandeur about the massive piers stretching to the distant choir and, although the nave appears to lack height, because the ribs of the lierne vault spring from a point lower down, the ridge is in fact almost as high as that at Canterbury.

The retro-choir and the first bay of the Lady Chapel are Early English (about 1200) but the rest of the Lady Chapel—making the overall length of the cathedral 169 m (556 ft)—is late Perpendicular. The floor of the retro-choir is paved more extensively with mediaeval tiles than any other church in the country. The presbytery with its fine reredos closing the eastern end was recast in the fourteenth century but the clerestory and timber ceiling are early sixteenth-century work.

There are unusually good wall paintings dating from about 1225 in the Chapel of the Holy Sepulchre off the north transept, and a number of chantry chapels, the finest of which is that of the cathedral's famous bishop William of Wykeham (1367-1404) in the nave. Amongst many furnishings of note are a black Tournai marble font of c. 1180 in which Henry III was baptised and, in the choir, the oldest set of canopied stalls in England of c. 1320 with small but lively misericords, and a stone Virgin and Child of c. 1340.

WEST and CENTRAL ENGLAND (Bristol, Chester, Coventry, Gloucester, Hereford, Lichfield, Oxford, Worcester)

This final group includes the red sandstone cathedrals of the west plus the new one at Coventry (see Chapter 9) and the more durable limestone trio of Bristol, Gloucester and Oxford. With the possible exceptions of Gloucester and Worcester, none are of the first rank and the red sandstone has weathered badly necessitating much refacing and consequent loss of texture. They include three abbeys and a priory, created cathedrals by King Henry VIII in 1541-42 (Bristol, Chester, Gloucester, Oxford).

Bristol. The cathedral at Bristol shares with Lübeck in North Germany and Toulouse in France the invidious position of being overshadowed architecturally by another church in the same city, in this case St. Mary Redcliffe.

Externally, with its north side felicitously facing College Green, the cathedral presents one of the flattest elevations of any English diocesan church, with low central and western towers and no clerestory. The reason for the absence of the latter is made clear upon entering as the aisles are carried up to the height of the central area, thus creating the country's only hall-type cathedral (apart from Guildford). Advantage

31

has been taken of this to provide the aisles with a unique form of vaulting in which transverse buttresses (like wooden tie-beams) are inserted above the arches, carrying miniature ribs which link them with the vault. A modern screen separates the nineteenth-century nave from the fourteenth-century lierne-vaulted Decorated choir. The Norman chapter-house of c. 1155, approached by an arched and vaulted vestibule, south of the crossing, is the finest example of the style in the country and amongst Bristol's other pleasures are the rare star-decorated tomb recesses, the oldest chandelier of 1460, choir stalls with twenty-eight misericords of c. 1520 and a late Saxon carving depicting the Harrowing of Hell.

Chester. Although one of England's more modest cathedrals, it nevertheless is superlative in one respect. The choir stalls, a magnificent canopied and pinnacled set with forty-eight misericords, all exquisitely carved, are the finest in England. Architecturally, the prize goes to the early thirteenth-century chapter-house with its attractive vestibule. The latter was part of the monastic buildings of which the fifteenth-century cloisters and the thirteenth-century refectory with wall pulpit also survive. The refectory is now part of the Cathedral School.

Also of the thirteenth century is the Early English Lady Chapel, the only part to have stone vaults.

The south transept dating from the fourteenth century is the largest in any English cathedral, having served once as the parish church of St. Osyth.

The building has suffered greatly from the softness of the sandstone used and from injudicious nineteenth-century restoration.

Gloucester. An impressive but somewhat ungainly Norman nave with a low vault of c. 1240 is married to some of the earliest Perpendicular work in the country; this new style was to set the fashion for the next one hundred and fifty years until the end of the mediaeval period. The funds obtained from the pilgrims to the shrine of King Edward II (see earlier) were used to remodel the eastern end of the Norman Benedictine abbey dating from 1089 to 1160, of which the crypt and chapter-house also remain.

The Norman choir was recased in the new Perpendicular style with a much-bossed lierne vault creating the effect of an immense panelled and traceried cage with a huge and slightly canted east window (the largest stone-traceried example in England so far as the area of glass is concerned). This was inserted between 1347 and 1350 and commemorates the fallen at the Battle of Crécy, which had taken place just before in 1346. Much of the glass retains its original silver, blue, yellow and red colours and amongst its small figures is one of a man playing a game like hockey.

The refashioning and rebuilding continued from 1331 (in the south transept where it started) to the end of the fifteenth century when the Lady Chapel was added and the style had reached maturity. Although one may have reservations regarding the clinical perfection of the skilled mason-work of the east end, the cloisters added in the third quarter of the fourteenth century and the tower erected in the 1450s are two of Gloucester's greatest assets. The glazed cloisters, with some of the earliest fan-vaults in the country, are complete with monks' lavatorium and carrels (recesses for their desks). The tower, clearly derived from Worcester, although nearly one hundred years later and over 9 m (30 ft) higher, is a spectacular example with a lovely crown but with somewhat repetitive decoration and excessive horizontal emphasis.

Furnishings include fifteenth-century canopied stalls.

Gloucester is the pre-eminent Perpendicular cathedral of the country and it is unfortunate that it gains so little from its site and that the close is so unduly cluttered.

Hereford. Apart from the weathering of its sandstone, Hereford cathedral suffered from the collapse of the western tower in 1786 which necessitated rebuilding part of the nave. In the process its character was altered and this is now an unconvincing mixture of Norman and Gothic, and one bay shorter. The present façade dates from 1902–08.

From whichever point the visitor looks the exterior is distinguished by the sturdy and noble central tower of about 1320, although from the distance it tends to be overshadowed by the taller spires of two of Hereford's other churches.

The other main external feature is the stately north porch; this is of two dates, the interior from shortly after 1300 and the exterior from 1516–35.

Internally, the outstanding part is the Decorated north transept of about 1250 with unusual triangular arches, clearly inspired by Westminster Abbey.

The Early English Lady Chapel is one of the oldest in the country and the retro-choir is of the same period.

Amongst many notable possessions are a chair, in which King Stephen is believed to have sat in 1138, the famous Mappa Mundi of c. 1260, early fourteenth-century choir stalls with one of the finest sets of misericords of this date in the country, a notable fourteenth-century canopied throne, the renowned chained library and the delicate tracer-ied canopy of the monument to Bishop Aquablanca who died in 1268. A smaller memorial of note is the marble bust believed to represent James Thomson who died in 1757, by the great French sculptor—Roubiliac—in the south-east transept.

Lichfield. The cathedral was besieged no less than three times during the Civil War of the mid-seventeenth century and pillaged and pro-faned by the Cromwellian soldiery.

It is therefore a much restored building, the central spire 79 m (258 ft) high having to be rebuilt in 1661-66 and again very largely in the eighteenth century. In the nineteenth century, the cathedral suffered a particularly thoroughgoing Victorian overhaul.

Nevertheless, it retains much of its charm, especially when viewed from the Minster and Stowe Pools, and the three spires—the only example in an English cathedral (*Ladies of the Vale*)—add grace to the picture from wherever one looks.

The much refaced (1885) west front, originally completed in 1293, except for the spires which followed in c. 1320-30, is elaborately decor-ated but the statuary is Victorian, the relief flat and the spires—less than 61 m (200 ft) high—are insufficiently lofty for the overall effect. A feature of particular interest is the wrought-ironwork of the scrolled hinges of the central doors, the upper pair being original 1293 work.

The nave, dating from about 1260-80, is distinguished by its excel-lent proportions although only 17 m (57 ft) high and the effects of the new Decorated style can be seen in the naturalistic leaf-carving of the capitals, which takes the place of the earlier stylised leaf type. The shafts are carried up from floor to vault, imparting a linear pattern so characteristic of English Gothic architecture.

A rare combination, however, for England is the continental hall-type Lady Chapel of 1320-1336 with its polygonal termination and nine tall windows filled with Flemish glass of the sixteenth century.

The chapter-house of 1249—an elongated octagon—is approached by a vestibule with a beautifully carved arcade. On the west side are the seats from which the feet of the poor were at one time washed. The capital of the central shafted pillar has four designs, each carried out by a different craftsman.

Furnishings and fittings are mostly Victorian but a monument of great charm is the memorial carved by Sir Francis Chantry to *The Sleep-ing Children* who died in 1812.

Oxford. The old Augustinian priory of St. Frideswide, which started as a nunnery in the eighth century, was made a cathedral in 1542 (another Henry VIII creation) after Cardinal Wolsey in 1524 had lopped off four bays of the nave to provide space for the Tom Quad of his Christ Church College foundation, of which the priory became the chapel. As a result the building is only 49 m (160 ft) long.

The priory had been rebuilt in transitional Norman style between 1158 and 1195 and this prevails in most of the building with the unusual arrangement of the triforium being contained in the main arcades. The Lady Chapel on the north side is attractive Early English and the spire (renewed) dating from about 1230 is the earliest one in stone in the country.

The glory, however, of Oxford Cathedral is the magnificent pendant lierne vault built over the choir in the late 1490s with the unique feature of stone lanterns hanging down from concealed arches. Each vault has a delightful star pattern with contrasting areas of light and shade.

The building is also fortunate in its fourteenth-century stained glass, especially in the St. Lucy Chapel where it includes many grotesques. The Latin Chapel has good fifteenth-century choir stalls. In addition, mention should be made of many excellent seventeenth- and eighteenth-century monuments.

Worcester. Perched above the north bank of the river Severn, Worcester has one of the most dramatic sites in the country and lovers of cricket are constantly reminded here, as at Adelaide in Australia, of the presence of the Cathedral.

Distance lends enchantment to the weathered sandstone exterior. The tower in particular, although refaced, is a noble sight from afar, finer even than that at Gloucester but not so lofty (60 m [196 ft] compared with 70 m [230 ft]). It was a rebuilding not carried out until 1374 after the original Norman tower had fallen in 1175.

Internally, from the Norman period, remain the impressive crypt (imaginatively used as a museum to illustrate the history of the church), and the only centrally planned chapter-house of this date in England.

The choir, eastern transepts and retro-choir begun in 1224 in the Early English style are the most notable parts architecturally of the interior, with rich mouldings and unstinted use of Purbeck marble and with the especial refinement of a two-plane triforium of exceptionally beautiful design.

As the nave is Decorated, except for the two western bays which are Transitional, and the tower is Perpendicular, all mediaeval styles are thus represented at Worcester.

Although the Victorian fittings are a great disadvantage, there are, to balance these, outstandingly good monuments including the famous marble effigy of King John, the magnificent chantry of Prince Arthur and fourteenth-century misericords (built into nineteenth-century stalls) which include a complete set of *Occupations of the Month.*

Apart from the chapter-house, monastic remains include cloisters (mostly fourteenth century) and refectory with a Norman undercroft.

The three western cathedrals—Hereford, Gloucester and Worcester—are noted for their annual Three Choirs' Festival.

NORTHERN IRELAND (Armagh, Belfast, Downpatrick, Londonderry)

Armagh. The ecclesiastical capital of Ireland, this is the seat of two archbishoprics. The two cathedrals, both dedicated to St. Patrick, who according to general belief started his missionary work here in 432 and founded a church in Armagh, reflect the differing traditions of the Roman Catholic Church and the Church of Ireland (Protestant). The Church of Ireland cathedral is a modest, sober and dignified building of cruciform shape with a central tower, dating mainly from the nineteenth century but with transepts going back to the second half of the thirteenth century. There are good monuments by the Flemish sculptors, Nollekens and Rysbrack and the French sculptor Roubiliac. The twin-towered Roman Catholic cathedral, built in the Decorated style between 1840 and 1904 of limestone, is an imposing and ornate building 68 m (225 ft) long, approached by a flight of seven steps and richly decorated with various marbles, mosaics and stained glass.

Belfast. St. Anne's cathedral, begun in 1898, is not yet completed and, because many people have had a hand in its construction, working to different styles, is a disparate but nevertheless impressive building. It is of basilican design and follows strict mathematical proportions (aisle walls half the height of the nave/clerestory walls, nave twice as wide as each of the two aisles, etc.) The floor of the baptistery is made of Irish marbles and these, together with mosaics, richly adorn the Chapel of the Holy Spirit. They are also used with maple in the nave floor which includes a distinctive stone from each of Ireland's thirty-two counties.

Downpatrick. A fine but ponderous Gothic design, the choir was drastically remodelled in 1798–1812. It is built chiefly of unhewn stone and has a lofty, embattled and pinnacled early nineteenth-century western tower. There are attractive pews in alternating curves and straight lines.

Londonderry. Like Armagh, it also has two cathedrals (St. Columb—Anglican, and St. Eugene—Roman Catholic). Both have lofty spires. Although St. Columb's nave dates from as late as 1628–33, it is still Gothic but the church was altered and restored in the nineteenth century (the tower and spire were rebuilt in 1805–34, and the chancel added in 1888). St. Eugene's spire dates from 1873.

SCOTLAND (Aberdeen, Dundee, Edinburgh, Glasgow, Inverness, Iona, Millport, Perth)

The episcopal church in Scotland has suffered much from religious strife, exacerbated by its allegiance to the Stuart cause during the eighteenth century. Many of the interesting buildings architecturally, such as Brechin, Dunkeld and particularly Elgin, are ruins or only partially usable and no longer rate as cathedrals. Most of the episcopal churches therefore are nineteenth-century structures.

Aberdeen. St. Andrew's Cathedral is a building of the nineteenth/twentieth century with a north aisle roof decorated with the arms of forty-eight American States and the west window commemorating the consecration of Bishop Seabury, the first bishop of the American Episcopal Church, which took place in a chapel nearby.

Dundee. St. Paul's has replaced Brechin as the cathedral church of the diocese although the bishop still takes as his title Bishop of Brechin. The building dates from 1852–55 and has a 67 m (220 ft) spire. The apsidal chancel has a reredos of Italian mosaics. Sir George Gilbert Scott was the architect.

Edinburgh. St. Mary's, dating from 1874–79, has a central 81m (276 ft) spire and is another Scott building.

Glasgow. St. Mary's is one more Scott church dating from 1870–71 with a 62 m (205 ft) spire of 1892–93, but the city has an ex-cathedral, St. Mungo's, which could justifiably claim to be Scotland's premier church architecturally. Located on one of the earliest Christian sites in the Kingdom, going back to its consecration as a burial ground by St. Ninian in 397, St. Mungo's has managed to keep its roof, unlike most Scottish mediaeval cathedrals, and is a fine example of thirteenth- or possibly early fourteenth-century work with richly shafted and moulded arcades, triforium and clerestory, the choir being the oldest portion.

Externally, the building suffers from the loss of its two western towers (in 1846 and 1948) but has a fine central tower with broach spire, 68 m (225 ft) high. The transepts do not project. Internally, the views both east and west are striking. Below is an extensive crypt or lower church (it is completely above ground) and the entrances from outside have attractive doorways. This lower church, 37 m (123 ft) long and nearly 19 m (62 ft) broad, is one of the finest examples of Scottish mediaeval architecture. At one time it contained the shrine of St. Mungo whose tomb is below the floor (he was buried there in 603) and became a leading centre of pilgrimage, no doubt bringing in much wealth.

Inverness. St. Andrew's, the mother church of the diocese of Moray, Ross and Caithness, was built in 1866–69 and is notable for its nave of polished granite and the oaken screen separating nave from chancel. The Angel Font was copied from one at Copenhagen Cathedral.

Iona. The ex-cathedral of Iona, built in the thirteenth century and famous for its associations with St. Columba, is much restored. The best features are the nave capitals and the carved doorway of the sacristy, dating from 1500. In the chancel, a polished stone kept behind a grille is said to be St. Columba's pillow.

Millport. Begun in 1849 and still incomplete, it is situated on Great Cumbrae Island and is the mother church of the diocese of Argyll and the Isles. St. John the Divine at Oban, dating from 1863–82, is co-cathedral.

Perth. Another product of the nineteenth century, Perth dates from 1850–90. It has a lofty Gothic nave and chancel separated by a stone screen carrying a rood. The baldacchino is of Cornish granite. It is the cathedral church of the diocese of St. Andrew's, Dunkeld and Dunblane.

WALES (Bangor, Brecon, Llandaff, St. Asaph, St. David's)

Until 1923, when Brecon was added, only Bangor, Llandaff, St. Asaph and St. David's had attained diocesan status. Welsh cathedrals have suffered more than most from war, neglect and heavy restoration, to which has to be added considerable damage from a landmine at Llandaff in 1942. Their origins, however, go back further than those in England, for Wales was the scene of missionary activity before St. Augustine came to Canterbury in 597. Bangor probably occupies the most ancient cathedral site in the British Isles.

Bangor. By the eighteenth century the cathedral had fallen into a very bad state and the building we see today is largely a nineteenth-century restoration by Sir George Gilbert Scott, who also carried out the work at Brecon, St. Asaph and St. David's. He rebuilt the western pinnacled tower and transepts originally erected in the sixteenth century whilst the eastern part with its tall Perpendicular window was left in the mixture of mediaeval styles in which he found it. The nave has six bays with octagonal columns. The lantern of the tower is supported by fine arches. There are good stalls.

Brecon. The main interest of Brecon Cathedral (once a Benedictine Priory) is the choir with its five lancets set above the reredos and its French-style vaulting. Externally, this church composes well from the north-east with its short battlemented central tower and steep-pitched roofs.

Amongst its furnishings are a fine Norman font of chalice design, richly decorated, a sixteenth-century wooden effigy of a young lady in the south aisle, and a unique thirty-cupped cresset stone, once used for lighting the church. This is near the south-western corner, where there is another stone probably used for the sharpening of arrows.

Llandaff. Despite all its vicissitudes, the cathedral has emerged as an interesting building with many unusual features both in its architecture and furnishings. The two western steeples are completely different in form, one a late fifteenth-century tower with an elaborate crown of Somerset type and the other a reconstruction after collapse with a tall octagonal spire of northern French type. The space between the steeples is taken up by a fine example of a west front of Early English design dating from about 1220, one of the most notable pieces of architecture in Wales.

Entry from the west leads down steps to the nave which is dominated by the concrete parabolic arch supporting the organ case and decorated with Epstein's sculpture *Christus* in unpolished aluminium. This provides an unimpeded vista to the sanctuary which previously was obstructed by a brass screen.

There are no transepts or triforium. The Lady Chapel, which is separated from the sanctuary beyond by a large arch surviving from the

Norman church, dates from the second half of the thirteenth century. There are also rich transitional Norman doorways dating from about 1170 on the north and south sides of the cathedral.

The attractive modern additions include the Rossetti Triptych (chapel in south-west corner), porcelain Della Robbia panels designed by Burne-Jones (chapel north of sanctuary), the John Piper window above the high altar and, especially, the decoration of the Lady Chapel.

St. Asaph. The victim of incessant warfare in the Middle Ages and a very poor diocese, this is the smallest of British cathedrals and the only one in Wales to be set on an elevated site. The choir is much altered Early English and the nave arcades, with square clerestory windows above, are Decorated; the central tower, only 28 m (93 ft) high, received battlements in 1714. The west window of six lights is noteworthy and there are fifteenth-century stalls. This is a modest sandstone church with a long history.

St. David's. Set on a promontory in a rocky moorland glen, this building is the most notable architecturally of Welsh diocesan churches, despite suffering from harsh eighteenth-century restoration and the need for further work in the nineteenth century.

Externally the view from the south-east shows it to best advantage with the aisles extended to embrace the western end of the Lady Chapel. The roof is low and flat and the central tower sturdy but lacking in grace. The building material is mainly a purple sandstone quarried in the area.

Internally, the cathedral slopes upwards to the choir and is distinguished by its nave arcades in transitional Norman style set on columns alternately round and octagonal. The timber roof above, with pendants hanging at the intersection of panels and rafters, is an outstanding example of late mediaeval work and there are other good roofs in the transepts and—fan-vaulted—in the chapel separating the presbytery from the Lady Chapel. The fourteenth-century pulpitum screening the nave from the choir is asymmetrical and the choir is an enclosed chamber with elaborate parapet and canopied canons' stalls; these have amusing misericords (one depicting what appears to be seasickness and another sciatica), all in oak of the late fifteenth century. The sedilia in the sanctuary are rare fifteenth-century examples of wood.

3
France

At the beginning of the mediaeval era, France was a small royal domain bordering the middle reaches of the rivers Seine and Loire, encompassed by powerful duchies and fiefs, nominally subject to but in fact independent of the king. Power lay in the hands of abbots and barons, and the great churches were abbeys. The cathedrals were relatively minor and there were none on the scale of Durham, Ely, Norwich, Peterborough and St. Albans in England.

From 1100 to 1137, the royal domain was governed by Louis VI, a wise ruler who concentrated on maintaining law and order in his small kingdom, aided by officials drawn from the middle classes and by his chief minister, the Abbot of St. Denis in Paris. This man, Abbot Suger, was responsible for the introduction of Gothic architecture into France, whence it spread to the whole western world. The exact origins of Gothic architecture are still debated but it seems probable that the pointed arch came from the Near East, where the absence of timber made straight lintels impracticable, and the advent of simultaneous Norman rule in Jerusalem, Sicily and England in the second half of the eleventh century may have been the channel through which the new style became known to Abbot Suger. In 1135, he embarked upon the rebuilding of St. Denis, the greatest abbey of the region, using the latest techniques of pointed arch and ribbed vaults, and, on 11 June 1144, the new wide portal, the enlarged choir and part of the nave were consecrated in the presence of Louis VII and his queen Eleanor—the first, even if only transitional, Gothic building in Europe.

Three years after the abbot had started work at St. Denis, Archbishop Henri Sanglier in 1135 began construction of a new cathedral at Sens, and it was not long before other prelates followed suit.

The reigns of Philip Augustus (1180–1223) and Louis IX (1226–1270) coincided with one of the greatest architectural flowerings in the history of art. Philip had made Paris into the cultural centre of Europe as well as the capital of France, had authorised and supported the University, which was founded in 1215, and built the cathedral of Notre-Dame. Scholars flocked from all over Europe to sit at the feet of Abelard and others, whilst the philosophy and thought of ancient Greece were made

41

available to the western world through contact with Spain, who had gained them from the Moors. The neo-Platonist school at Chartres became famous but the philosophical and art schools of Paris, which had become predominant by the end of the twelfth century, were to have an even greater impact upon Euopean civilisation.

The effect upon the evolution of Gothic architecture was enormous. Already the main lines of development had been set by earlier building. Particularly instructive, because it has been little altered, is the cathedral of Laon (started in about 1160) which set the pattern. Its three western portals deeply recessed and richly sculptured were to become a feature of the transept portals at Chartres; the western rose-window with arcade above was to be perfected at Notre-Dame de Paris; the bell-towers were models for the towers of Rheims and the use of flying buttresses was an essential element. Laon, however, is unusual for France in having a flat east end instead of an apsed ambulatory with radiating chapels and also in the number of its towers, a characteristic of many Rhineland churches, also seen at Tournai in Belgium.

The process of building in Gothic was hastened by a series of devastating fires, which destroyed or badly damaged the old Romanesque cathedrals.

France, at this period of its history, was experiencing a wave of religious fervour which affected all classes. Stimulated by the Crusades and the bringing back of relics, such as the head of John the Baptist (Amiens) and the tunic of the Virgin Mary (Chartres), and by the determination of high-minded bishops, aided by the king, to throw off the arbitrary ascendancy of the abbots, everyone from the highest in the land to the humblest contributed not only money but their labour, harnessing themselves to wagons to haul the stones to the site and bringing food to the workers.

In some cases, as at Chartres, reconstruction was not total but in the majority of cases, including most of the finest, such as Amiens, Bourges and Rheims, the cathedrals were completely rebuilt. As the technique of using flying buttresses above the aisles to counterbalance the weight of the vaults was developed, these were carried up ever higher, to reach the prodigious altitude of 48 m (157 ft) at Beauvais. At the same time, walls became less massive and window-space larger, letting in more and more light and providing large surfaces for the glass-maker to instruct the illiterate with pictures in rich colours which they could understand and which embraced the whole range of mediaeval thought.

Building did not continue without interruption as lack of funds caused many stoppages. Nevertheless, the cathedrals took far less time to build than later ones and between 1050 and 1350, which admittedly overlaps the Romanesque phase, eighty cathedrals were constructed. But the destruction and havoc wrought by the English during the Hundred Years' War between 1337 and 1453 were not conducive to large-scale building and, by the fifteenth century, the creative urge had died.

Of this prolific output, Amiens, Beauvais, Bourges, Chartres, Notre-Dame de Paris and Rheims must be accounted as some of the great architectural masterpieces of the world. But preceding these, St. Etienne de Sens, the earliest of the French Gothic cathedrals, repays study in view of its influence on later buildings.

Sens. Begun only three years after Abbot Suger started work at St. Denis, the choir of Sens was completed and consecrated in 1164. The nave was built between 1175 and 1180 so that the main structure of this Gothic cathedral was in existence well before the end of the twelfth century. The collapse of the southern tower, however, in 1268 did much damage to some notable sculpture carved on the western façade but enough remains to appreciate its quality, especially the statue of the patron saint St. Stephen (St. Etienne) on the *trumeau* (central column) which is similar to the statue columns at Angers and Chartres. Particularly enjoyable features of the decoration are the scenes in the medallions which include a strange legendary figure from Libya called a sciapod who uses his huge foot for protection from the heat of the sun.

Flying buttresses were added in the thirteenth century to counterbalance the thrust of the domed vaults but these, by later French standards, are not particularly high, being just over 24 m (80 ft) from the floor. The nave, however, is comparatively wide 13 m (44 ft).

Much later but nevertheless striking additions to the fabric are the fifteenth-century transept fronts with elaborate Flamboyant tracery in the rose- and other windows which are filled with early fifteenth-century glass, rich and glowing on the north side, softer and less easily seen on the south. The oldest glass, however, is the early thirteenth-century medallion glass in the north bay of the ambulatory which, among other themes, includes the story of Thomas à Becket.

Amiens. A series of fires culminated in a blaze that reduced the fourth of Amiens' cathedrals to ashes in 1218. There was nothing left to inhibit the architect, who in this case is known from an inscription in the nave labyrinth (Robert de Luzarches), from erecting a completely new edifice, except to preserve the church of St. Firmin (which lay where the north transept now stands) until the relics of this local saint could be transferred to the cathedral. This led to the unusual sequence of the nave

Magi medallion, Amiens, France.

being built (1220–36) before the choir, which was finished in 1269. Chapels were added later and the upper parts of the towers (although never completed) were erected in the second half of the fourteenth/ fifteenth century but, mostly, this vast cathedral was built in the space of fifty years, an astonishingly short time.

As a result, we have inherited a building uniform in style, constructed when French Gothic architecture was at its peak, of noble and harmonious proportions and one which must be considered as the classic Gothic cathedral. The length of the nave (133 m [438 ft]), its great height (42 m [138 ft]) and the elaborate tracery of the choir, together with the openwork of its triforium, create a tremendous impact, as it is uncluttered with tombs except for the outstanding bronze monuments on the floor of the nave to the founder bishop, Evrard de Fouilloy and his successor, Geoffroy d'Eu, both of which date from the thirteenth century. The bases are, in each case, of one piece.

The noble west front, although less clearly designed than that of Notre-Dame de Paris and inferior in its upper part, is richer in sculpture (erected between the early 1220s and 1236, and restored in 1843-47). This embraces a complete collection of mediaeval iconography including medallions, showing little known symbols of the hermetic science, and is dominated by the unforgettable *Beau-Dieu* or figure of Christ on the *trumeau* of the middle porch.

Unfortunately, the masons in their desire to provide the maximum window space did not allow for the humidity of the Picardy climate and in time the iron framework corroded, causing the glass to fall out; most of the mediaeval glass that remained was lost in a fire during storage so that Amiens lacks this great adornment found at Bourges and Chartres and many other French cathedrals.

As some compensation, Amiens has one of the finest sets of choir-stalls in France, carved with consummate skill and artistry between 1508 and 1522 during a period of prosperity; only those at Auch are comparable. They include many local scenes illustrating life in Amiens at that time. Although the stalls are much later than the structure, they harmonise with it and there are no subsequent additions or alterations to disturb the contemplation of this Gothic masterpiece.

So attached did the citizens of Amiens become to their cathedral, that when the Revolutionaries threatened it they rallied to its defence and it was saved.

Beauvais. Situated about halfway between Amiens and Paris, this cathedral suffered the effects of two fires, the first in 1180 and the second in 1225, a few years after Amiens had been devastated in 1218. The bishop and canons, with the Amiens design in mind, determined to build a diocesan church without equal. Unfortunately, they had neither the financial nor material resources to do this and they had no relic to attract pilgrims. Shortly after work started on the choir in 1227 the vault collapsed and again in 1284. By the end of the fourteenth century only the choir and one bay of the nave had been completed, and the chaos created by the Hundred Years' War made further progress impossible. It was not until 1500 that construction was begun of the transepts which, as at Sens, were built in the Flamboyant style with great rose-windows being completed by the middle of the sixteenth century. But then, instead of proceeding with the nave, the bishop and canons conceived the crazy scheme of erecting over the crossing a tower and spire which was to break all known records and structural laws and, on Ascension Day 1573, the inevitable happened and the whole steeple fell to the ground.

By great self-sacrifice, funds were eventually found to buttress the choir but the religious wars at the end of the sixteenth century put paid to any further work and, when a Protestant bishop took possession of the see, the western end of the choir was shored up in 1605 and no further work has been done on the structure, so that Beauvais has an immense soaring choir and apse with transepts but nothing else, except for one bay of the planned nave.

Bourges. The early history of Bourges Cathedral, dedicated to St. Etienne, is obscure but, unlike so many of the Gothic cathedrals of France, it does not seem to have been rebuilt as a result of a fire. The first mention is in a manuscript recording a farewell sermon by Archbishop St. William in 1209 which would indicate that construction was then in progress. It had many predecessors going back to the third century, and Louis VII was crowned in 1137 in its immediate forerunner.

Situated almost in the centre of France, this magnificent building was consecrated in 1324, having taken some hundred years to erect, and the great west window, or *housteau*, was not completed until the end of the fourteenth century at the expense of one of Bourges' greatest citizens, Jean le Bon, who became Duke of Berry shortly after the dedication and to whom we owe the whole of the cathedral's vast west front with its unique five instead of the usual three portals. He built his own monument in the crypt and a chapel for himself larger than La Sainte-Chapelle in Paris. On New Year's Eve 1506/07 the northern tower, only recently completed, collapsed and subsequently the northern portal of the west front was rebuilt in a style different from the others. The decoration of the west front later suffered grievously, first from the Huguenots and then during the Revolution, when St. Etienne was only left standing because it was estimated that it would cost more to pull down.

Sited on the highest point of the town and built out at the east end over a crypt necessitated by the ground falling away, the cathedral, with a huge buttressing pier on the south side, sits astride the hill creating an impression of great bulk; the interior, without transepts or tribune galleries and with double aisles continuing without interruption from the nave through the choir and round the ambulatory, is sensational. Many people have likened the aisles to great avenues lined with tall trees, and the combination of space and height is nowhere in France so ingeniously contrived. Whereas the columns of Notre-Dame de Paris are 6 m (21 ft) high, those at Bourges, made to look slender by shafts rising directly to the springing of the vaults, are 17 m (55 ft) high carrying the nave to a height of 37 m (123 ft); the inner aisles are over 21 m (69 ft) above the floor so that we see a harmonious upward gradation of levels from the outer aisles to the inner ones and eventually to the nave, which is filled with light.

But perhaps Bourges is most renowned for its stained glass and, despite the vandalism already mentioned, also the depredations of the clergy who actually removed some of the choir glass in 1760, we are able to study stained glass from its peak in the thirteenth century, and probably coming from the same workshop as contemporary glass at Angers, Chartres and Le Mans, to the fifteenth and sixteenth centuries, and even to its decadence in the seventeenth century. The oldest glass is in the outer ambulatory and the choir in the form of medallions; higher up are strange, fierce-looking tall figures. To this must be added early fifteenth-century glass in the crypt, once in the Duke of Berry's private chapel, and fifteenth/sixteenth-century glass in other chapels.

Of the sculpture, some mediaeval work survives in the west front, especially in the Central Portal of Judgment but it is not the equal of that at the other great cathedrals.

Chartres. During the night of 9/10 June 1194 lightning destroyed the cathedral except for the crypt and the west front including the bases of the two towers. The building (begun in 1134 after an earlier fire) had been the occasion for a spontaneous upsurge of religious exaltation, aimed at providing a worthy sanctuary for the statue of the Virgin and the Sancta Camisa or tunic, believed to have been worn by her, which had come from Constantinople and been presented to the church. The rich had contributed their wealth and the poor their muscle; all classes worked together to haul the stone, the timber, the food and drink, prepare the mortar and cook the food for the builders so that, at night, there was a great encampment of helpers around the site.

Undaunted, the work began again after the calamity of that June night. The west front, including the Royal Portal, was incorporated into a new cathedral which, as the crypt still remained, had to follow the foundation structure of the older building with the addition of transepts. By 1220 the 130 m (427 ft) long and 37 m (121 ft) high nave was completed; the great porticoes on the north and south sides with their noble statuary (over seven hundred statues remain) were added between 1220 and 1245 and the whole cathedral was filled with exquisite glass. Within sixty-six years, on 24 October 1260, all was ready for dedication in the presence of Louis IX (St. Louis) and his family.

This building has come down to us substantially unaltered with most of its sculpture and glass intact; the only additions to the original plan are a sacristy north of the choir, the Chapel of St. Piat at the east end increasing the overall length to more than 152 m (500 ft), and the Vendôme Chapel south of the nave. Between 1507 and 1513, the elaborate 115 m (377 ft) high Flamboyant spire was added to the northern tower creating a striking but harmonious contrast with the perfectly plain hollow pyramid rising to 106 m (349 ft) on the southern tower, erected three hundred and fifty years earlier in 1160. Later, the Revolutionaries mercifully confined their attentions to the plate and the furnishings and did not harm the sculpture and the glass.

The masterly architecture, the vivid and varied sculpture and the survival of practically all the original glass, combine to create at Chartres a sublime building.

Notre-Dame de Paris. Work on Notre-Dame was started in the year 1163. The moving spirit was Bishop de Sully who, aided by Louis VII, was able to advance building swiftly although to this day the name of the architect is unknown. The choir was ready for consecration in 1182, the nave was built between 1180 and 1200 and the magnificent five-stage west front, with its three portals, gallery of kings, rose-window, the arcade linking the twin towers and the towers themselves, was erected between 1200 and 1245. The gallery of twenty-eight kings of Judah and Israel, which was once thought to represent kings of France, is modern and the famous gargoyles, portraying so graphically the sins of man, were installed by Viollet-le-Duc during the restoration of 1845 to 1864, replacing earlier animals which had been destroyed or become eroded with time. Of the three portals, the tympanum and the panels of the Door of the Virgin have fortunately survived and depict one of the most moving representations of the *Life, Death and Crowning of the Virgin,* a popular theme in French mediaeval art. The panels show the *Signs of the Zodiac* linked with the *Occupations of the Month,* another very common theme, and are worthy of close examination.

In the middle of the thirteenth century, the transepts were extended and the opportunity taken to insert large rose-windows over 12 m (40 ft) in diameter making, with the line of narrow windows below, a glazed area nearly 18 m (60 ft) high topped by a gable. There are notable porches below. At the end of the century, construction began on the great east end or chevet with double tiers of flying buttresses producing, with Le Mans, built earlier between 1217 and 1245, the two finest eastern terminations to be seen in France. The buttresses of the Notre-Dame chevet have been likened alternatively to the oars of a Roman galley or to the legs of a huge spider but, whichever simile is drawn, the chevet is a *tour de force*.

The central spire is modern but retains the mystical symbolism of the Apostles, preceded by the beasts of the Apocalypse, coming down to evangelise the world.

This fine piece of architecture can be viewed easily from all sides of its island site.

Rheims. Helen Henderson in her book *The Cathedrals of France* wrote a harrowing description of Rheims as she saw it in 1923—'its floor . . . still piled with the débris of its gashed and shattered beauties'. The visitor today, therefore, must marvel that this once-tangled mass of wreckage has been restored to its present state and that this superb piece of architecture can still present its unique west front to the world with its deep portals and its glorious sculpture, executed at the zenith of the mediaeval sculptor's art.

Being the coronation cathedral of the French kings, the richness of the decoration, which is carried up into the gables above the portals, round the great rose-window, over the walls and buttresses, in the niches of the towers and even behind the façade, is unsurpassed. Within, we see for the first time in France beautifully executed naturalistic leaf adornment both on the capitals and around the famous panels on the inside west wall.

Inevitably, the cathedral lost most of its thirteenth- and fourteenth-century glass during the war devastation and only fragments remain in the choir and in the north aisle of the nave. In this respect, therefore, Rheims must suffer in comparison with Chartres which has emerged unscathed from all the perils of war, revolution and insensitive restoration. But, architecturally, it is arguable whether Rheims is not the finest cathedral in the world. Despite the main structure taking one hundred years to build, it shows remarkable unity of design and purity of form, each succeeding architect following faithfully the pattern set by his predecessor.

Work started in May 1211 after an all-consuming fire in 1210, a few years earlier than Amiens, but as construction took such a long time Rheims was able to reflect later developments, notably by incorporating window tracery. The choir was completed in 1241 but ran the builders into considerable financial trouble so that the nave and west front were not finished until 1311. The open-work towers were erected in the fourteenth century but the northern tower did not receive its last touches until 1427. The building measures 138 m (454 ft) inside and the nave rises to 38 m (124 ft).

The sculpture was executed mainly between 1241 and 1290 but there is earlier carving on the portals of the north transept. The style of the figures varies, three different workshops being involved. The sculpture portrays *Christ's Life and Ministry* on earth and amongst the many vivid impressions the visitor receives are the smiles on the faces of two of the angels, one aptly termed *The Smile of Rheims*, the Annunciation scene in which the other angel appears, the Visitation, the figure of Joseph with its sly expression looking no doubt very much like a French peasant of the time and the *Presentation of the Holy Child by His Mother to Simeon*.

The west front of Rheims, whilst perhaps lacking the classic lines of Notre-Dame de Paris must be one of the most elegant in the world and one which would repay hours of study.

Amongst the beautiful panels inside on the west wall with their frame of natural foliage, there are many New Testament saints and a particularly striking representation of a knight receiving the chalice, an image to the mediaeval mind of the ideal of a crusader.

As at Amiens, the citizens stoutly defended their cathedral against the destructive ideas of the Revolutionaries, but war was more than they could contend with and it is only the solidity of the work of the mediaeval mason that enables us to see the building as it is today.

The following are descriptions of some of France's other cathedrals.

NORTH and EAST (Auxerre, Châlons-sur-Marne, Dijon, Langres, Metz, Strasbourg, Toul, Troyes and Verdun)

Auxerre. Built over an eleventh-century crypt, this distinguished building has some fine but mutilated sculpture on the west front and south transept portal. The choir is early thirteenth-century. The nave was completed in 1344 but the northern tower was not finished until the sixteenth century. The particularly fine apsidal chapel has skilfully executed vaulting. Thirteenth-century glass (restored) remains in the clerestory.

Châlons-sur-Marne. Basically of the second half of the thirteenth century, the first two bays of the nave and the west front date from 1628–1634. Towers flank the choir, and there is a notable thirteenth-century rose-window in the north transept and plate tracery.

Dijon. A former abbey church dating from the turn of the thirteenth century, the austere twin-towered Gothic façade retains a twelfth-century Romanesque porch. The crossing is surmounted by a 92 m (305 ft) spire, rebuilt in Flamboyant style in 1896 and the interior is well-proportioned.

Langres. Built in Transitional twelfth-century style with a fine Romanesque choir, the façade is Classical eighteenth-century. There is a notable Romanesque door to the chapter-house, remains of thirteen-century cloisters and a fine alabaster fourteenth-century Virgin (*Notre-Dame la Blanche*).

Metz. Oriented from north to south, construction of this building took from 1220 to the early sixteenth century. The exterior is sombre due to the use of brown stone. The nave rises to 42 m (137 ft) and the impressiveness of the interior is enhanced by the raised sanctuary.

Strasbourg. The most notable cathedral of this group, positioned on the borders of France and Germany, Strasbourg reflects the influences of both countries. The tower, with curious ladder-like supports in its upper stages, and the spire, which resembles a pine-cone, were the work of German architects and, except for Rouen, are only exceeded in height by the tower and spire of Ulm, Germany, and the spires at Cologne with which they have close affinities. The sculptural decoration, on the other hand, draws its inspiration from the great northern French cathedrals and, although falling short of them in execution, is full of interest (many of the original figures are housed in the nearby museum). Built of a local pinkish sandstone (*grès de Vosges*), Notre-Dame de Strasbourg, in the same way as Notre-Dame de Paris, gains greatly from its island site. The smooth texture, however, of the refaced stone detracts from one's pleasure.

The cathedral incorporates a crypt dating from the first quarter of the twelfth century, the transepts were begun in the middle of the same century whilst the nave was built between 1235 and 1275, and the west front between 1277 and 1339. The statuary includes the famous *Vices and Virtues*, and the *Wise and Foolish Virgins*, but these slender figures lack the nobility of the sculpture further north. Beside the south transept portal are the well-known figures of the Synagogue, blindfolded with broken staff and looking disconsolate, and the Church, proud with Cross and Chalice upheld.

Toul. The choir, flanked by towers as at Châlons-sur-Marne, dates from 1221–1260, the transepts from the fourteenth/fifteenth century and the Flamboyant west front from the latter part of the fifteenth century. There are attractive thirteenth-century cloisters to the south and the west front towers terminate in octagonal lanterns, as at Tours.

Troyes. The present cathedral's predecessor was destroyed with most of the city in a disastrous fire of 1188. Reconstruction did not start until 1228 and for various reasons, notably the difficulties of the site and the Hundred Years' War, took a long time to build, the northern and only tower not being completed until 1580. The church is especially striking for its large window area and the upward sweep of the tall clerestory windows, filled with stained glass, from the thirteenth century in the choir, and from 1498–1501, when the art underwent a revival, in the nave. The construction is extraordinarily light.

The west front, begun in 1506, is notable, despite being denuded of its statuary by the Revolutionaries.

Verdun. The sanctuaries at each end are not apsed but the building is Rhenish in having double transepts. Begun in the second half of the eleventh century, it was much altered in the fourteenth and eighteenth centuries and severely damaged in World War I.

CENTRE and SOUTH-EAST (Aix-en-Provence, Clermont-Ferrand, Grenoble, Lyons, Nevers, Vienne, Viviers)

This group includes cathedrals (Clermont-Ferrand and Nevers) showing northern influences and others (Grenoble, Lyons and Vienne) which have a distinctive regional flavour. Aix-en-Provence and Viviers reflect the style of the south. Although none of these churches is outstanding they have many interesting features.

Aix-en-Provence. A sixth-century baptistery stands beside the cathedral which has an aisleless thirteenth-century nave and beautiful late twelfth/early thirteenth-century cloisters with coupled marble columns having richly decorated capitals. The fifteenth-century west front has fine doors and there is a notable triptych of 1475/76 by Nicholas Froment.

Clermont-Ferrand. Built of black volcanic stone with twin western towers in its nineteenth-century façade, this cathedral is the clearest example of the northern influence. Begun in 1248, the choir was completed in 1344, followed by the nave and transepts. The fourteenth-century rose-windows have original stained glass.

Grenoble. The large tower forms a porch and the transepts date from the eighteenth/nineteenth century. There is a thirteenth-century tabernacle.

Lyons. The choir dates from 1165/80, and the nave and transepts from the thirteenth century. The west front with its short stocky towers (as at Vienne) was erected in the fourteenth century. The cathedral lost its statuary in 1562 but retains an interesting set of bas-reliefs on the splays of the portals. The choir was completed at the end of the fifteenth century and in 1486 the celebrated Bourbon Chapel was added.

Nevers. The cathedral dates mostly from the first half of the fourteenth century although the richly ornamented twin bell towers are fifteenth-century. It is double-apsed and resembles Bamberg, Germany, in that one apse is Gothic and the other Romanesque.

Vienne. The nave dates from 1107/48 and the choir is thirteenth-century. The west front is similar to that of Lyons but later (fifteenth-century) and retains its statuary. The window area is large.

Viviers. The porch and west front are twelfth-century and the radiating chapels are fourteenth/fifteenth-century. There are Gobelin tapestries.

SOUTH (Albi, Bayonne, St. Bertrand de Comminges, Bordeaux, Carcassonne, Dax, Marseilles, Narbonne, Oloron-Ste Marie, Perigueux, Perpignan, Rodez, Toulouse)

Albi. The most famous and the strangest of this group is the brick-built cathedral of St. Cecilia, looking more like a fortress than a church, and dominating, with its donjon-type tower and flat roof, the town below. It was designed to withstand attack, which it frequently suffered, and reflects the cruel and violent character of its founder bishop, Bertrand de Castanet, a Dominican, who was Grand Inquisitor.

Started in 1282, it took just over one hundred years to build but was not consecrated until 1480, by which time the 78 m (255 ft) high tower had been completed. The white stone Flamboyant porch on the south side which serves as the main entrance was added between 1529 and 1535. The delightful screen which embraces the choir and the charming furnishings within were begun about 1500. Apart from the porch the exterior is bare of ornament and there are no transepts or western façade. The bare cliffs of brick with narrow slits for windows (the lower windows are nineteenth-century insertions) offered no foothold for attackers and the thick walls of the tower are only pierced by loopholes.

Inside, the design provides for one huge hall 30 m (98 ft) high and 14 m (45 ft) wide without aisles and with chapels set between the abutment piers, but the choir-screen is full of exquisite carving and reflects more nearly the gentle character of the cathedral's patron saint. Around the choir are vivid stone statues of Old Testament figures, wonderfully expressive, and the choir-stalls are decorated with a frieze of angels. The entire surface of the interior was painted by Italian artists in the sixteenth century.

Bayonne. Erected between the thirteenth and sixteenth century in northern style (the nave after the fire in 1310), this is one of the finest cathedrals in the south-west. The second tower and spires were added to the western façade in the nineteenth century. The interior is well-proportioned and there is sixteenth-century stained glass and a thirteenth-century sanctuary knocker on the north door. The cloisters on the south side are fourteenth-century.

St. Bertrand de Comminges. Dramatically sited on a Pyrenean peak, with superb views from the cloisters, this hall-church has notable choir stalls including delightful detail of St. Matthew and St. Luke. Fine Renaissance woodwork can be seen in the choir-screen, rood-screen, pulpit, organ-case and retable. Behind the high altar is the mausoleum of St. Bertrand. The eleventh/twelfth-century cloisters have interesting capitals and are noted for the pillar of the four Evangelists in the west walk.

Bordeaux. This shows a contrast of modest eleventh-century aisleless nave and ambitious fourteenth/fifteenth-century double-aisled northern type choir with noble chevet. The fine and richly ornamented tower has a short truncated spire. There is good thirteenth-century sculpture on the north portal and fourteenth-century work on the Porte Royale (also on north side).

Carcassonne. Like Bordeaux (although on a smaller scale) this is a mixture of Romanesque eleventh-century nave and Gothic choir (1300–1320), the latter without ambulatory or radiating chapels but with a two-stage elevation and southern in character. The thirteenth/fourteenth-century stained glass is some of the best in the south and the statues on the piers at the choir entrance are of good northern quality.

Dax. Originally Gothic, this was rebuilt in 1656–1719 in Classical style after being razed by fire and completely restored in 1894. There are domed towers and good thirteenth/fourteenth-century portals within the church and also a charming early sixteenth-century *St. Anne and the Virgin* clinging to her mother's cloak (in the choir).

Marseilles. The old cathedral is twelfth-century. The new cathedral is a huge Romanesque/Byzantine structure, erected between 1852 and 1893, and rising to 70 m (230 ft) under the cupola.

Narbonne. The choir, constructed of hard limestone in 1272–1319, is on a grand scale (51 m [170 ft] long, over 40 m [131 ft] high), only exceeded in altitude by Amiens and Beauvais). The nave however was never built because city walls prevented extension. It is northern in style with cloisters on the south side and many works of art.

Oloron-Ste Marie. The cathedral is twelfth-century but the choir was rebuilt after fire in the fourteenth century. The outstanding Romanesque portal at the foot of the steeple, largely thanks to hardness of Pyrenean marble, has survived invasions and religious wars. Subjects depicted include hunting wild boar, fishing, salmon-smoking, and cheese-making.

Perigueux. One of the largest of south-western France, this was rebuilt in Byzantine style with a domed vault after being destroyed by fire in 1120 and drastically restored in 1852–1901. It is of Greek cross design (unusual for France) and the cloisters are half Romanesque and half Gothic.

Perpignan. This hall-church was begun in 1324 and consecrated in 1509. Attached to the south side is a square tower with an eighteenth-century campanile of wrought-iron. The fifteenth- and seventeenth-century retables, particularly the one behind the high altar, are renowned. The fourteenth-century wood-carving of Christ in the south-west chapel is particularly moving.

Rodez. Started in 1277 but not completed until the sixteenth century, the severely plain west front is of about 1500. The 90 m (295 ft) north tower of red sandstone, one of the finest in the region, was started in the fourteenth century but dates mainly from the first half of the sixteenth century with a Renaissance top reminiscent of those at Tours. The choir stalls have amusing misericords, such as ducks with intertwined necks and little girls with strange hairstyles.

Toulouse. St. Etienne's Cathedral is of mixed styles, architecturally inferior to Toulouse's harmonious Romanesque church of St. Sernin. Lack of funds prevented the new nave being built to conform with the northern-style choir as intended, so that the original of 1209 is on a different axis. A second nave aligned with the choir dates from the nineteenth century.

WEST (Angers, Le Mans, Limoges, Poitiers, Tours)

This group embraces churches of the southern hall-type (e.g. Angers), in which emphasis is on space rather than height, and others of the northern type (Le Mans, Limoges, Tours), in which verticality is stressed.

Angers. The cathedral shows the development from the northern-type three-ribbed vault to the southern domed vault with ribs stretching upwards. The aisles were removed in 1125/48 and the two western and central towers date from the first half of the fifteenth century.

Le Mans. The nave, dating from the eleventh/twelfth century, has been retained and, in 1217/54, the magnificent choir with chevet rivalling that of Notre-Dame de Paris, was added. Although the transepts were raised, the difference in height between the nave and the choir is disquieting. The beautiful mediaeval glass ranks with that of Bourges and Chartres, one piece representing the Ascension in the south aisle of the nave being considered the oldest in existence.

Limoges. Begun in 1273, Limoges is unusual in having a campanile-type tower linked to the nave by a narthex. The western part of the nave and the façade were not completed until 1876/88. The St. Jean Portal on the south side, built of very fine granite between 1516 and 1530 in Flamboyant style, has a slim gable stretching up to the rose-window. The stained glass in the choir is twelfth-century; that in the aisles and the transepts is thirteenth- and fourteenth-century.

Poitiers. This is the earliest example of hall-type construction in European cathedrals. The west front with towers outside the aisles gives a façade of great width. The flat east end is unusual for France. The stained glass in the choir is twelfth-century; that in the aisles and transepts is thirteenth/fourteenth-century.

Tours. Started in 1236 and taking three hundred years to build, it is consistent in style. It has a refined external appearance with Renaissance tops to its two western towers. The large rose-window forms one composition with lancets below (as at Bourges). The thirteenth-century stained glass is outstanding. A touching monument on the right of the choir to the infant children of Charles VIII and Anne of Brittany was completed in 1505.

NORMANDY and BRITTANY (Bayeux, Coutances, Quimper, Rouen, Sées)

The cathedrals of Normandy and Brittany have a distinctive regional flavour. Many have central towers—a feature not common elsewhere in France—regal (Coutances), striking (Rouen); these are both lantern towers. Some are crowned with nineteenth-century accretions, such as the very tall and unsuitable iron spire at Rouen (at 156 m [512 ft] the tallest in France) and the unfortunate copper 'bonnet' at Bayeux. Others have twin western towers, some also crowned with spires as at Quimper (modern) and Sées (restored stone).

Bayeux. The Romanesque arcades are distinctive for the exotic carving in the spandrels set against a diapered background of plaited basket-work. The triforium, deeply moulded in the choir, and the vaulting is Gothic. The heads of four bishops are painted on the choir vault. The world-famous tapestry in the adjoining museum once lined the walls of the cathedral, the length of which it matched.

Coutances. Built over a fairly short period between 1218 and 1274, Coutances shows great purity of line and elegance of proportion. The semi-circle of coupled columns around the apse is particularly satisfying and, although the absence of decoration gives a somewhat cold aspect, the view upwards to the lantern from the crossing is spectacular. Externally, as at Bayeux where the view is helped by the cathedral being sited on an open slope, the chevet with many turrets and flying buttresses is outstanding. The west front is similar to Bayeux in having towers of four receding stages capped by very pointed spires, which at Coutances rise to 78 m (256 ft).

Quimper. Built in the thirteenth to fifteenth centuries, this is one of the finest Gothic buildings in Brittany. The spires on the twin western towers are modern and the portals are richly sculptured but worn. The design is consistent but the choir is not aligned with the nave. There are stained glass, altarpieces and statues of the fourteenth/fifteenth century, episcopal tombs and a sumptuous modern high altar.

Rouen. The cathedral at Rouen is also an outstanding example of Gothic architecture although not as symmetrical in design as Coutances. It dates mainly from early thirteenth century but the façade, except for the northern tower (St. Romanus), which goes back to the twelfth century and is one of the oldest parts, is much later. The façade itself was built in 1509/30 and the magnificent southern tower, called the *Tour de Beurre* (because it was erected from funds obtained by granting indulgences on the eating of butter and cream during Lent) is a little earlier (1485–1507). North and south portals of the late thirteenth/ fourteenth century are famous for their profusion of carving but the west front is enriched almost to excess.

The fine interior has a long nave of eleven bays, divided exceptionally into five horizontal divisions, and a double-aisled choir. The beautiful Lady Chapel contains notable monuments, especially those to the de Brézés and to Cardinals Georges I and II of Amboise. The stained glass ranges from the thirteenth to the sixteenth centuries and includes the thirteenth-century window of St. Julian the Hospitaller in the north ambulatory of the choir and the famous piece stating that 'Clement of Chartres made me', the only example of glass of this period to be autographed, thus linking it with the great Chartres glass-makers. The choir stalls date from 1457/69.

Rouen was the chief French cathedral casualty of World War II but has been well restored.

Sées. Despite many vicissitudes, including shifting soil, this is an unspoilt thirteenth/fourteenth-century cathedral. The western façade, flanked by twin 70 m (230 ft) high towers with stone spires, is pierced by a huge porch. The three-storey nave has round columns and the choir and transepts are exceptionally well lit. The transepts have notable rose-windows with thirteenth-century stained glass (the northern depicting the Incarnation and the southern, the Redemption). There is also old glass in the ambulatory chapels.

4
Germany (West)

German cathedrals go back to the beginnings of Christianity in that country. Trier started as a square basilica of the fourth century and Aachen as the private chapel of Charlemagne in the eight/ninth century —its octagonal shape and mosaic decoration being modelled on San Vitale at Ravenna, Italy. However, the main development of Carolingian architecture was towards long double-ended churches with apsed choirs, transepts at each end and circular towers flanking the apses. This was continued during Ottonian rule (863–1024) leading to the multiplicity of towers characteristic of Rhineland Romanesque.

Although German churches of this style were rather bare inside, political affinities with northern Italy resulted in the exteriors being ornamented with blind arcading, and dwarf galleries beneath the eaves and round the towers. In the north, twin towers with a wall between or a single massive tower were common.

All this gave a distinctive German flavour to their Romanesque cathedrals and the style persisted well into the thirteenth century, some time after England and France had turned to Gothic. Limburg, not completed until 1242, retains a Romanesque exterior although the interior was altered later in the thirteenth century to resemble the Gothic cathedral of Laon in France. Similar to Minden Cathedral in the north, it is an example of the late transition from Romanesque to Gothic.

When Gothic eventually arrived, the use of double-ended apses was not completely discontinued, for the western apse at Bamberg is Gothic, but German Gothic was not—as in England and France— evolved from Romanesque so much as imported ready-made from France. The French style is apparent in the large cathedrals of Cologne, Frankfurt, Freiburg, Regensburg and Ulm which were basically products of the fourteenth century but, being buildings conceived on the grand scale and designed to impress (the Archbishop of Cologne was for many centuries a Chancellor of the Holy Roman Empire), it was a long time before they were completed, in most cases not until the nineteenth century. Frankfurt, Freiburg and Ulm, however, differ from French practice in concentrating upon a single large west tower accompanied by a comparative slimness at the base and the clerestories of earlier Gothic churches often begin immediately above the nave arcades without triforium or tribune between them.

By now, decoration and sculpture were playing a much bigger part. Painting and carving in stone showed minute attention to detail and realism of expression, compelling but sometimes carried to excess.

Ulm is a so-called *hallenkirche* or hall-church and, by the fourteenth century, German Gothic had taken an independent turn by sacrificing verticality to open spaciousness and carrying up the height of the aisles to match that of the nave and choir. This was not, however, a German invention for the first cathedral to this design had been started at Poitiers in France as early as 1162. Visually, the effect was to create oblique vistas rather than to carry the eye upwards or to the high altar at the east end. Transepts and ambulatories were omitted and wall space increased so that once again the walls could bear the stress of the vaults directly without buttresses. Vaulting ribs disappeared and, instead, mouldings having no structural function were used in the form of stars or nets as decoration. Stained glass ceased to have mystic significance and became purely decorative whilst the areas of windows were reduced and they were frequently taken up from floor to ceiling. This spatial design lasted until the end of the Gothic period.

Internally, there was a great increase in the number of movable ornaments—elaborate altarpieces with wooden superstructures filled with figures and with folding coloured doors, paintings and, on special occasions, tapestries. Fonts and pulpits became more elaborate and choir-stalls were enriched with beautiful carving, at which the German workers in wood were particularly skilled.

There was little limestone available for building and the use of sandstone, lava and other less durable materials has led to frequent refacing, with the result that the German penchant for restoration is made even more apparent by surfaces lacking the patina of old age. Red sandstone from quarries in the upper Rhine was used for Mainz, Speyer and Worms cathedrals, although this is combined with grey limestone in the interior of Mainz. In the north, brick was the prevailing material and this is also found further south in the Frauenkirche at Munich and the walls of Ulm.

The Renaissance period, coinciding with the Reformation turmoil, had a very limited effect on cathedral architecture, but Baroque, starting from about 1660, had a much greater impact although Fulda in the east is the only entirely Baroque example.

In the nineteenth century, on a tide of nationalism and Romanticism, Cologne, Regensburg and Ulm were at last completed and, as in England and France, there was much tampering with other cathedrals including,

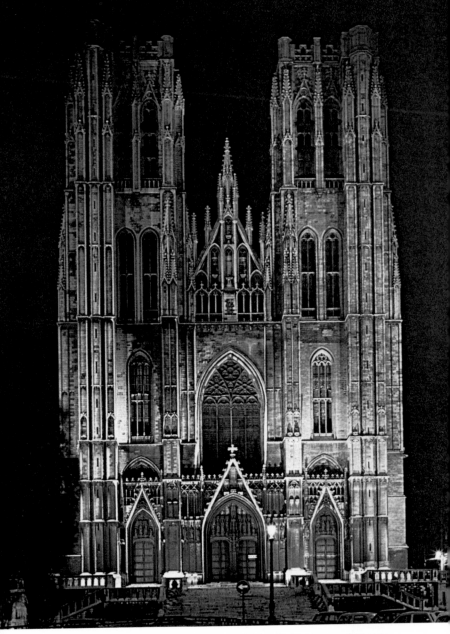

1 The Cathedral Church of St Michael, Brussels, Belgium. Better known as St Gudule, and built on a hill overlooking the centre of the city, the western façade shows strong English influence and has been likened to that of Westminster Abbey.

2 The Collegiate Church of St Paul, Liège, Belgium. Was raised to cathedral status in 1801. The vista eastwards up the well-proportioned nave leads the eye to the polygonal apse with its tall mid-16th-century stained glass windows.

3 St Paul's, London, England. The western façade is of Renaissance style with Baroque towers. The pediment bears a relief of the Conversion of St Paul and a statue of the saint stands on the apex. Behind is the superb dome and lantern.

4 Durham, England. The view of the cathedral set high above the waters of the River Wear is a thrilling architectural experience. Its dominance is underlined by the red-roofed house in the foreground.

5 York, England. The richly decorated western towers with crowns of open battlements and eight pinnacles enclose a large central window with striking flowing
tracery. The towers were built during the middle of the 15th century.

6 Lincoln, England. The central tower, heightened early in the 14th century, is the loftiest mediaeval example in England. The lead-sheathed timber spire, believed to have reached a height of 160 m (524 ft) was blown down in a gale in 1548.

7 Peterborough, England. The fan vaulting of the retro-choir is similar to that of King's College, Cambridge and probably by the same designer. There is decorative panelling richly cusped beneath the windows and stone seats below.

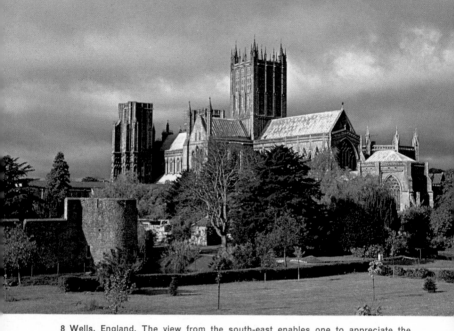

8 Wells, England. The view from the south-east enables one to appreciate the harmony of the much-pinnacled central tower and the beauty of the setting.

9 Winchester, England. The west front, dating from the second half of the 14th century, has the largest window in the cathedral. The porches are unusually low.

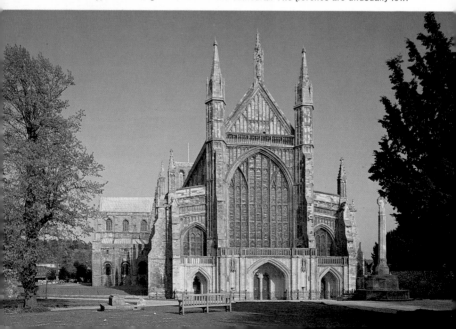

10 Bristol, England. The unique vaulting of the choir aisles has struts to transfer the thrust of the main vaults to the exterior buttresses and each bay has its own ribbed vault. The window symbolises the work of the Holy Spirit.

11 St David's, Wales. Of the tower, which collapsed in 1220, only the lowest stage of the unbuttressed crossing tower remains. The original pitch of the roof can be seen. The middle and top stages date from the 14th and 16th centuries.

12 Exeter, England. The magnificent vault stretches from end to end of the cathedral in an uninterrupted sweep. The numerous tierceron ribs spring from the same points as the main ribs.

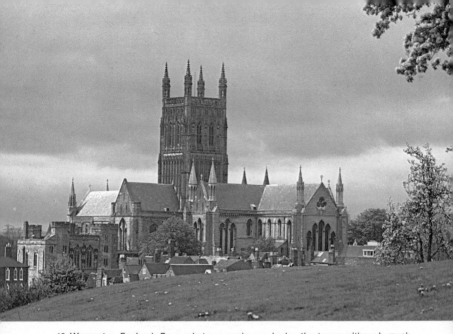

13 Worcester, England. From whatever angle one looks, the tower, although much re-faced, is a noble sight, beautifully proportioned and with a fine crown.

14 St Albans, England. The length is only exceeded in England by Winchester. The 19th-century stone west front contrasts with the Roman bricks of the tower.

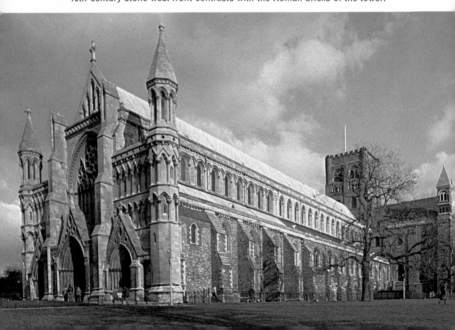

15 Norwich, England. The view from the cloisters shows the five-stage elevation of the main fabric. The cloisters, which were burned down during a riot of 1272, took well over a hundred years to rebuild but show surprising uniformity of style.

16 Salisbury, England. The superlative tower and spire were erected fifty years after the main structure had been completed. The spire is not only the loftiest in England but can claim to be the most graceful in the world.

17 Canterbury, England. The south-western tower dates from 1424–34 but the matching north-western one was not erected until 1832. The porch contains modern statuary dating from 1860 commemorating famous people in the history of Canterbury.

18 Chichester, England. Behind the high altar hangs one of the cathedral's contemporary works of art – the tapestry designed by John Piper and made near Aubusson in France. Beyond is the fine retro-choir.

19 Ely, England. The octagon is a *tour de force* built to take the place of the central tower which fell in 1322. The exterior walls are of stone but the central lantern is of wood faced with lead; the vertical members consist of large oak beams.

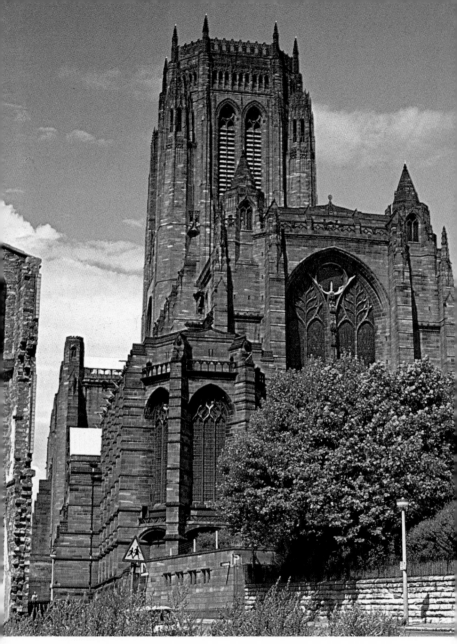

20 Liverpool, England. The Anglican cathedral is one of the most impressive buildings of the 20th century, with a majestic tower rising to 101 m (331 ft), octagonal at the top. The east window with Decorated-style tracery depicts women of the Bible.

21 Coventry, England. The view from the south-west shows the interesting saw-tooth arrangement of the windows and the Epstein statue of St Michael and Lucifer.

22 Guildford, England. The cathedral stands on a hill away from the centre of the town. The exterior, made of bricks from local clay, has clean crisp lines.

23 Rheims, France. The Coronation Cathedral of the kings of France is renowned for the richness of its decoration. The west front with its deep portals is one of the finest in the world and is unsurpassed for its glorious sculpture.

24 Chartres, France. The masterly architecture, the exquisite glass and the noble sculpture combine to make this perhaps the finest cathedral in the world. The two spires blend although widely separated in date.

25 Notre-Dame, Paris, France. The west front is a superbly proportioned and harmonious five-stage façade with deep, richly sculptured portals and a fine rose window. Strong horizontal lines balance the upward thrust of the towers.

26 Albi, France. The eastern end, bare cliffs of brick with narrow slits for windows,
underlines the fortress character of this forbidding exterior. The lower windows
are 19th-century insertions.

27 Rouen, France. The upward view to the central lantern gives a dramatic sensation of space. It is a bold construction rising 50 m (164 ft) from the floor to the keystone of the vault.

28 Amiens, France. Built mainly during the peak of French Gothic, uniform in style, this classic cathedral is of noble, harmonious proportions.

29 St. Bertrand de Comminges, France. The west walk of the cloisters, rebuilt in the 15/16th centuries, has a pier decorated with figures of the four Evangelists.

30 Florence, Italy. The Duomo is the second largest church in Italy after St. Peter's, Rome. Giotto's campanile contrasts with Brunelleschi's splendid dome and lantern, which took fourteen years to build and reaches a height of 106 m (348 ft).

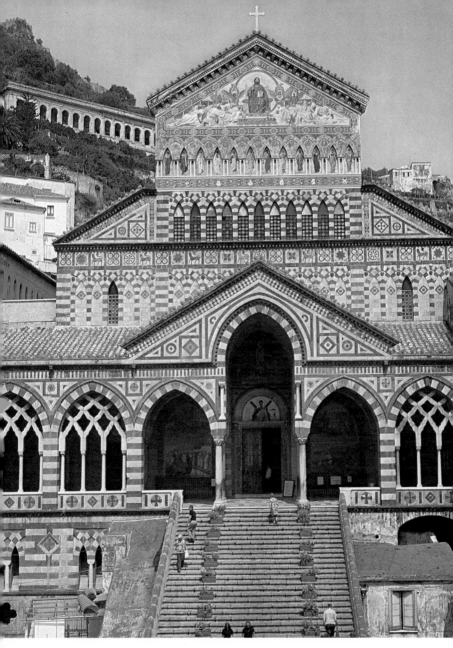

31 Amalfi, Italy. The façade is a 19th-century reconstruction to the original design
impressively sited at the head of a flight of steps. The sharply pointed arches to
the atrium are constructed of alternate layers of black and white stone.

32 Murano, Italy. The two-tiered apse with arcaded galleries of the Basilica of SS Maria e Donato is a fine example of the Byzantine Romanesque style found in the Veneto/Ravenna area. The campanile is a handsome structure.

33 Messina, Italy. The cathedral was almost entirely rebuilt after an earthquake in 1908. The 60 m (196 ft) bell-tower carries an astronomical clock, believed to be the largest in the world.

34 Cefalu, Italy. The 12th-century mosaic of Christ Pantocrator (Creator of All Beings) in the apse vault dominates the chancel.

35 Pisa, Italy. The serried tiers of blank arcading with fifty-four small marble columns is typical of Pisan Romanesque. The leaning tower serves as a belfry.

36 Cefalu, Italy. The cathedral, built of a golden-hued stone during the first half of the 12th century in fulfilment of a vow, has tall transepts pierced by large oculi (round openings) at the base.

37 Aachen, Germany. The 14th-century choir was modelled on the Sainte-Chapelle in Paris. Each of the windows is 26 m (84 ft) high with modern glass depicting the Life of the Virgin, her Assumption and the Consecration of the Cathedral.

38 Limburg, Germany. The seven-towered and turreted cathedral stands command-
ingly above the River Lahn. It is an example of the transition from Romanesque
(lower parts) to Early Gothic (upper parts), the latter modelled on Laon in France.

39 Cologne, Germany. The largest cathedral in Germany did not receive its spires and nave until the 19th century. The finest part is the apsed east end, dedicated in 1322, with tall windows which fill the whole of the space between the shafts.

40 The Cathedral of the Assumption, Zagorsk, Russia. The five huge domes in blue and gold picked out with stars symbolize Christ and the four Evangelists.

41 The Cathedral of the Assumption, Vladimir, Russia. Originally built as a single-domed church in 1158–61, it was enlarged after a fire and given another four domes in 1185–89.

42 The Cathedral of the Intercession, Moscow, Russia. Better known as St Basil's, and situated in Red Square outside the Kremlin, it is a monument to victory over the Kazan Tartars. Each tower contains a chapel and is decorated differently.

43 Sofia, Bulgaria. The cathedral was built as an expression of gratitude to the Russians by the Bulgarians for freeing them from Turkish domination and is dedicated to a Russian general. The exterior is distinctive for its domes and arches.

44 St Gallen, Switzerland. This Baroque Swiss cathedral has its principal façade at the east end flanked by towers with cupolas capped by lanterns.

45 Elvas, Portugal. Rebuilt in Manueline style in the 16th century, the massive western tower has an open belfry and a large recessed portal. The cathedral presides over the main square with its attractive chequer-work pavement.

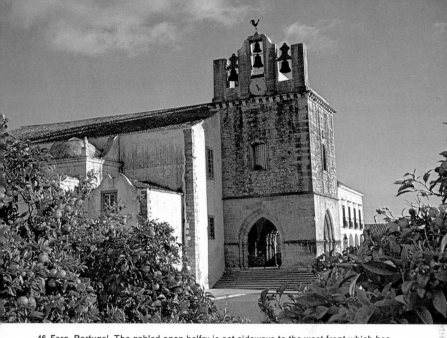

46 Faro, Portugal. The gabled open belfry is set sideways to the west front which has a tall porch surmounted by a bare upper storey.

47 Silves, Portugal. The Gothic cathedral, built of a local reddish stone, is unusual in that the transepts are higher than the apse which is crowned by merlons.

48 Burgos, Spain. This massive cathedral is distinguished externally by its fine 55 m (180 ft) high central lantern, dating from the mid-16th century, and its lovely skyline of twenty-two pinnacles.

49 Segovia, Spain. The cathedral is a late Gothic building of the 16th century. The much-pinnacled eastern end rises dramatically in mounting stages to the central dome with seven radiating chapels leading off the apse.

50 Seville, Spain. This largest of mediaeval cathedrals has a low profile without towers. The former Moorish Giralda belfry tower can be seen to the right.

51 All Saints' Cathedral, Nairobi, Kenya. With its twin Scottish-type saddleback towers, occupies a position outside the city centre in attractive gardens.

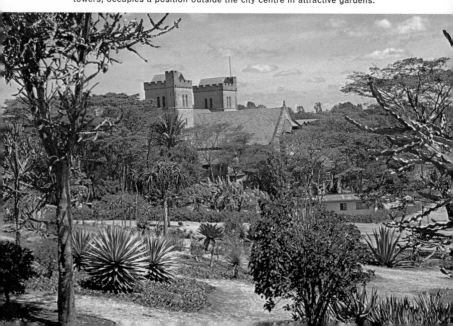

52 Salisbury, Zimbabwe Rhodesia. The cloisters, added after World War 2, are a pleasing feature of this mother church of Mashonaland. Construction started in 1913 and was completed in 1964. The north-west bell-tower dates from 1962.

53 Melbourne, Australia. The elegant central spire of this notable cathedral is well seen from the south-east. The towers and spires were not added to the 19th-century building until 1937–39.

54 New York, U.S.A. The fine portal with bronze sculpted doors is a worthy entrance to the most famous Roman Catholic cathedral in the U.S.A.

55 Tromsö, Norway. Although not episcopal, this striking modern church, so much in tune with its setting, is popularly called 'The Cathedral of the Arctic'.

at Speyer, the replacement of the eighteenth-century west front by an uninteresting flat façade.

NORTH (Bremen, Brunswick, Hildesheim, Lübeck, Minden, Münster, Paderborn, Ratzeburg, Schleswig, Soest)

Although most of these cathedrals had Romanesque beginnings, only Brunswick, Hildesheim and Soest remain essentially eleventh/twelfth-century whilst Hildesheim has had to be reconstructed after war damage and Soest is completely restored inside. Minden, Munster, Paderborn and Schleswig are mainly thirteenth-century and all are hall-churches, the style having started earlier in the north. Munster and Paderborn show the transition from Romanesque to Gothic but at Bremen, which took longer to build, the whole range of mediaeval styles from Romanesque to Late Gothic is apparent, although Bremen was rebuilt in the sixteenth and again in the nineteenth century.

Lübeck, founded in 1173 by the formidable Henry the Lion, Duke of Saxony (who was also the moving spirit behind the building of Brunswick, where he is buried), and Ratzeburg both underwent a complete transformation in the fourteenth century.

These northern churches, none of which are outstanding as cathedrals, lack the refinements of their central Continental counterparts and, particularly in Westphalia, reflect the more austere character of the people. They often present a gruff exterior typified in the so-called *westwerk*, a fortified western façade flanked by towers or having a single large tower, seen also across the border at Maastricht in the Netherlands. Apart from defence considerations in these disturbed areas, they are an early manifestation of the German desire for external height and the towers of Brunswick, Schleswig (which also has a fine spire), Bremen and Lübeck (spires) dominate the flat countryside for miles around.

In general, the interiors are more impressive than the exteriors, although the latter are sometimes enhanced by attractive porches and picturesque cloisters whilst Minden has a notable western façade.

There are many decorative features and furnishings of note which are included in the following summaries.

Bremen. The twin western towers have disproportionately large Rhenish caps (i.e. diamond-shaped roofs resembling a bishop's mitre). Fan-vaulting is found in the north aisle and Gothic stalls in the southeast chapel. The sixteenth-century carvings on the organ balustrade include figures of Charlemagne and Willehad, first bishop of Bremen, carrying a model of the cathedral. The crypt at the west end of about 1120, with carved Romanesque capitals, contains a notable thirteenth-century bronze font.

Brunswick. Of 1173–1195 with a typical *westwerk* façade, the interior is double-aisled with north aisles in Flamboyant style. There is a seven-branched candelabrum in the chancel and an impressive mid-twelfth-century crucifix in the north aisle (*Christ Clothed*). The tomb of Henry the Lion and his wife Matilda is in the nave and the large main crypt contains tombs of Guelph princes.

Hildesheim. A double-ended Romanesque building, the interior was remodelled in Baroque style in about 1720. Notable features are the magnificent bronze doors of 1015 (copy in the Victoria and Albert Museum, London), a huge eleventh-century chandelier, an unusual thirteenth-century font borne by four figures symbolising the rivers of the Apocalypse and an eleventh-century bronze column in the south transept depicting the *Life of Christ*.

Lübeck. A massive and very early brick church, this was converted into a Gothic *hallenkirche* in the fourteenth century. It suffered much from bombing which has necessitated bracing the 120 m (394 ft) high western spires—which are considerably out of the vertical, especially the north-west one—with massive iron girders.

The impressive interior has Romanesque piers whitewashed throughout. The bronze font dates from 1455 and the huge figure of Christ on the rood beam, from 1477.

The cathedral is overshadowed by Lübeck's Marienkirche, an exceptionally fine brick edifice, the builders of which deliberately set out to surpass the episcopal church.

Minden. The finest of the northern cathedrals, Minden has a beautiful Romanesque façade surmounted by a *westwerk*. The satisfying interior has tiered Rhineland-type arcading in the chancel. There is an outstanding Romanesque crucifix (eleventh-century) and a painting of the Crucifixion (1480), a rose-window, thirteenth-century statues and Baroque furnishings.

Münster. This early thirteenth-century (Transitional) hall-church has double chancels and double transepts. In the south porch around the inner doorway there are thirteenth-century statues. A 1520 altarpiece can be found in the south transept and a 1540 astronomical clock in the ambulatory. The fourteenth-century cloisters on the north side have a thirteenth-century bust of St. Paul. The Chapel of Holy Sacrament is to the left of the entrance to the cloisters.

Paderborn. The massive single western tower of this hall-church is the town emblem. The paradise porch (north) has mid-thirteenth-century statuary. From the atrium north of the chancel, the cloisters open. These contain a funerary chapel of Westphalian counts with an attractive altarpiece of 1517 and the well-known *Three Hares Window*. St. Bartholomew's Chapel to the north was built in 1017 by Byzantine masons. The famous portable altar of 1100 is in the Treasury.

Ratzeburg. In a beautiful setting on an island in parkland, this twelfth-century building is of brick with an attractive south porch. There is a notable Crucifixion altarpiece (1430) and Romanesque and Gothic choir stalls.

Schleswig. This large hall-church of brick with a fine spire was built in 1888–94. There are picturesque cloisters on the north side. The famous high altar by Hans Bruggemann (1514–21) is one of the largest carved altars in Germany with three hundred and ninety-two figures. The tomb of King Frederick I of Denmark is by the noted Dutch sculptor Cornelis Floris (1555).

Soest. The powerful west tower with two tiers of Romanesque openings (the lower merely slits) was once used as an armoury.

WEST (Aachen, Cologne, Frankfurt, Limburg, Mainz, Speyer, Trier, Worms, Xanten)

This is the heartland of Germany where, as might be expected, many of its finest cathedrals are to be found. They range from the delights of Xanten (sadly damaged during the 1939–45 War) to the showy magnificence of Cologne and span the thousand years from the ninth to the nineteenth centuries. The ninth-century domed chapel at Aachen served as the Palatine Chapel of the Emperors and was the place of their coronation from 813 to 1531. Mainz, Speyer (founded by Emperor Conrad II between 1024 and 1030) and Worms were all imperial cathedrals. The Archbishop of Mainz, like the Archbishop of Cologne, held for many centuries the office of Chancellor of the Holy Roman Empire.

Aachen and Trier have many relics and Trier, which started as part of a Roman palace in the fourth century, shows on its north and south sides the various stages of construction—the two original basilicas dating from 324–348 in the middle, Archbishop Poppo's eleventh-century extension to the west and the twelfth-century polygonal chapel (masked by a domed Baroque chapel) to the east.

Mainz and Speyer suffered from a succession of fires and, together with Worms, felt the full weight of French arms in 1689 which did immense damage and again in 1793 during the French Revolution. All this plus drastic nineteenth-century restoration seriously impairs one's pleasure. Worms, the least restored of the three, retains the texture of its warm sandstone and is the most enjoyable.

Limburg carries one into the Gothic age. Cologne, Frankfurt and Xanten are all completely Gothic buildings, not having been started before the middle of the thirteenth century. Cologne and Frankfurt are imposing buildings befitting the great conurbations which they serve. Cologne in particular, the largest church in Germany, commands by its sheer bulk, but neither is the equal of the great French cathedrals upon which they were modelled and they are only partially mediaeval. They were finally completed on a tide of nationalist enthusiasm in the nineteenth century.

Aachen. The ninth-century domed octagon is surrounded by fourteenth/fifteenth-century chapels and a two-storied ambulatory, to which was added a choir in the fourteenth century; this was modelled on the Sainte-Chapelle in Paris with thirteen windows each 26 m (84 ft) high (modern glass). The combination of Carolingian octagon and Gothic choir is unique but not particularly harmonious. Treasures include two golden reliquaries (Mariaschrein and Karlschrein) dating from the first half of the thirteenth century, a pre-mediaeval pulpit or ambo decorated with six ivory carvings, a coronation chair, Pala d'Oro golden altar frontal and bronzes of the tenth/eleventh century.

Cologne. The nineteenth-century west front is elaborated with numerous gables. Open-work traceried spires are 157 m (515 ft) high and the nave is 45 m (148 ft) high. Fine statues completed in 1322 are to be found against the choir piers and of c. 1385 in St. Peter's Portal. Excellent carving on the arms and misericords of the choir stalls was also completed in 1322. Five stained glass windows in the north aisle of about 1500 depict scenes from the lives of St. Peter and the Virgin. Behind the high altar is the twelfth-century Magi's Shrine, the cathedral's greatest treasure, containing relics of the Magi presented by

Emperor Frederick Barbarossa in 1164 to the archbishop.

Frankfurt. The main external feature is the tall Gothic central tower with its gabled octagonal upper storey complete with dome carrying a lantern and spirelet. The aisled hall-church has wide transepts, and there are fine fourteenth-century choir stalls.

Limburg. Magnificently positioned on a rock overlooking the river Lahn, the seven towers/turrets include one over the crossing capped with a small spire. The polychromed interior is unattractive. The font and Kurzbold tomb are of c. 1220.

Mainz. Of the two chancels, the western has wide transepts and a fine tower over the crossing, but the eastern is simpler. The very plain interior has a 28 m (93 ft) high nave of red sandstone and grey limestone. The floor of the choir is 2.5 m (8 ft) above the nave. There is an elegant fifteenth-century chapter-house, early thirteenth-century Gothic sculpture, fine imperial/episcopal monuments and a very impressive *Entombment of Christ* (c. 1495) carved in stone. The pewter font of 1328 has delicate figured ornament and the Rococo choir stalls are good.

Speyer. The longest Romanesque church in Germany, the main interior feature is the eleventh-century crypt with groined vaulting supported on arches of which voussoirs are cut alternately in pink and white limestone. A thirteenth-century tombstone of Rudolf of Hapsburg stands at the entrance to a vault containing the tombs of eight German Roman Emperors. The beautifully proportioned raised transepts have an octagonal dome and lantern tower. There is early groined vaulting in the nave and aisles.

Trier. Like Mainz and Worms, the ancient cathedral at Trier is a double-ended church, with a severely plain western façade, flanked by towers and conical-roofed stair-turrets, much as it looked when built in the eleventh century. Apart from some tracery in the openings of the southern tower, which is taller than the pyramid-roofed northern one and has a splay-footed spirelet, the only decoration is very shallow tall blind arcading and open galleries. There was a thorough restoration of the cathedral between 1891 and 1910 and the interior was newly decorated in 1907.

Among furnishings in the Baroque interior, one may single out the altarpieces, the fine Romanesque tympanum in the south aisle and the monuments to Johann III von Metzenhausen, who died in 1540, and to

Richard von Greiffenklan which are good examples of German Renaissance work.

In the north-west corner of the attractive cloisters, dating from 1220–30, stands a beautiful statue of the Virgin (the *Virgin of Malberg*).

Worms. Typical of Rhineland Romanesque design, the exterior of the west chancel, not completed until about 1230, is one of the best examples of this style. There are spirited Romanesque carvings on the sills of the three large east windows, a fine twelfth-century statue of Christ inside the south portal and an interesting early carving of *Daniel in the Lions' Den* in the first chapel on the right. There are eight imperial tombs below the chancel, Gothic sculptures in the north aisle and Baroque choir stalls.

Xanten. One of the finest Gothic buildings in the Lower Rhine but retaining its Romanesque western façade with twin towers, this was built between 1263 and 1519. There is a double-aisled nave, sixteenth-century cloisters and altarpieces, a choir-screen of 1400 and choir stalls of c. 1300.

CENTRAL and SOUTH (Augsburg, Bamberg, Freiburg, Freising, Fulda, Munich, Passau, Regensburg, Schwäbisch-Gmünd, Ulm)

This mixed group shows every style of European architecture except Classical, and ranges from the double-ended design common in the Rhineland (Bamberg) to the Baroque exuberance of Fulda and the prestigious self-assurance of Ulm's mighty 160 m (525 ft) high steeple, the tallest in Christendom. As one would expect in this largely Catholic area, Baroque is much in evidence. It is one of the richest areas for fine statuary. There is much mediaeval stained glass, including, at Augsburg, the oldest glass in Germany. Altarpieces and imposing doorways add to the pleasure of visiting these cathedrals, some of which also have attractive cloisters.

Most of these episcopal churches are mid to late mediaeval. Two Danube cathedrals, Regensburg and Ulm, are purely Gothic but the spires are nineteenth-century additions.

Augsburg. Founded in 995, this was rebuilt in Gothic style in the fourteenth century. The bronze doors have eleventh-century reliefs. The cathedral is double-aisled with twelfth-century windows in the south clerestory and paintings by Holbein the Elder on the nave altars. The cloisters are late Gothic.

Bamberg. A Transitional two-apsed building, founded in 1004, the eastern apse is raised on a terrace. The outstanding sculpture includes Adam and Eve on the south-east portal, Church and Synagogue figures in the Princes' Portal and, inside, an intensely-expressive face of Elizabeth in *The Visitation* and the famous equestrian *Rider of Bamberg* (completed 1237). There are tombs of Emperor Henry II and Pope Clement II, the only pope to be buried in a German cathedral, and fine choir stall carving.

Freiburg. This is perhaps the finest of the Gothic cathedrals but the nave is modest with poor windows. The single open-work tower has a traceried spire rising to 114 m (377 ft) (a model for later nineteenth-century steeples). The choir took from 1354 to 1513 to build and is taller and more impressive than the nave. The ambulatory has fan-vaulting. It is richly furnished, the high altarpiece of 1512–16 being especially notable.

Freising. The Romanesque fabric has been re-decorated inside in Baroque style. The twelfth-century crypt has a curious column entirely covered with carvings of strange beasts. The stalls have Flamboyant canopies carved with busts of early prince-bishops. The altarpiece in gilded wood, decorated with a copy of Rubens' *The Woman of the Apocalypse*, is impressive.

Fulda. Rebuilt in 1704–12 in Baroque style, there are twin towers, a central dome, and a crypt of St. Boniface, relics of whom are contained in the Treasury, including a codex with which he tried to ward off murderers.

Munich. The Frauenkirche was built of dull red brick in 1468–78, the onion domes (symbol of Munich) were added in 1525, making the towers 99 m (325 ft) high. The unassuming white hall-type interior has a reticulated vault. The stained glass is of 1392. The mausoleum of Emperor Ludwig of Bavaria is beside the south tower.

Passau. On the highest point of the town, the east end dominates the square. The dome over the crossing is shaped like a German steel helmet. Late Gothic, it was converted after a fire into Baroque in 1668–78. It is

View from twin towers of Ulm, Germany.

spacious with altar paintings and numerous seventeenth/eighteenth-century monuments.

Regensburg. A cathedral city since the eighth century, the present building, although striking in scale, is not well-proportioned and lacks refinements. It is unusually austere for a Roman Catholic cathedral. Although the All Saints Chapel of 1155–64 with murals covering the walls and domed ceiling survives from an earlier church, Regensburg was built mainly between 1275 and 1530 but the double-steepled west façade was not completed until 1859–69. The porch is original, with carved and figured portals. The statuary is beautiful, especially St. Peter and the Visitation group in the central doorway and, inside, the Angel Gabriel and Annunciation of about 1280. There is excellent fourteenth-century stained glass in the three chancel windows.

Schwäbisch-Gmünd. This was built in the fourteenth-century by Heinrich of the famous Parler family of architects who came from this city. There are no towers and a huge roof with a two-tiered east end. The interior is a classic example of hall design with Intricate vaulting in the chancel. There is much statuary on the Renaissance choir stalls and in the radiating chapels, especially notable being the early fifteenth-century *Holy Sepulchre Watched by the Three Marys*.

Ulm. This is a grandiose but not particularly sensitive building of the fourteenth/fifteenth century with an 1844–90 steeple. Crisp in outline, the twin-towered east end was completed in the late fourteenth century. The choir stalls by Jorg Syrlin (1469–74) are an outstanding example of the wood-carver's art. The hall interior is without transepts and the aisles have star-shaped lierne vaulting. The pulpit is surmounted by a secondary pulpit with a Flamboyant baldacchino for the Holy Ghost (the invisible preacher).

5
Italy

The cathedrals of Italy are many and varied, reflecting the divided state of the country after the collapse of the Roman Empire. There are two hundred and seventy-five of them and, as J. W. Franklin points out in *The Cathedrals of Italy*, the number of towns which have, or once had, cathedral status is three hundred and forty-one. Several therefore are quite small and not noticeably different from the larger parish churches.

This multiplicity had its origins in the administration of the Roman Empire which was based upon the fact that everyone lived in towns. The early Christian Church, after it became officially established in the fourth century, followed the same pattern and in each town a bishop became the head of a local church which only later came under more central control.

This tendency was encouraged by Italy's history after the fall of Rome. Subject to frequent invasion and racked by dissension, the country dissolved during the Middle Ages into a confusion of city-states and communes, every one aspiring to have a worthy cathedral church of its own.

Stylistically, although Italy was subject to many influences, the dominating one was the classical legacy of ancient Rome. The Romanesque style which developed out of this lived on much longer in Italy than in most other countries and, with only a limited use of the Gothic styles which prevailed north of the Alps and which were never taken seriously, formed the basis of the fine flowering of the Renaissance, when the virtuosity of Italian artists and architects redounded throughout Europe.

The provincial variations are very marked. The basilican form (long-aisled nave with apse at the east and narthex or portico at the west), especially the magnificent mosaic decoration, lingered on in the Ravenna and neighbouring areas where the Byzantine Eastern Empire made a come-back after the invasion of the Goths under Theodosius. Apulia and Sicily, despite frequent and devastating earthquakes, provide delightful examples of the happy marriage between Saracenic and Norman designs which grew out of the successive conquests by these two peoples.

Gothic made its greatest impact in Lombardy and Tuscany where the imposing cathedrals of Florence, Milan, Orvieto and Siena demonstrate its forms in gables, buttressing and vaulting but the stress is more on decoration than architecture, the latter becoming a screen for the former and it is not the Gothic of soaring vaults, steeply pointed arches and traceried windows of the North. The exuberance of ornament and colour which adorn the façades of Orvieto and Siena are alien to French and British taste and have no counterpart in Spain. Florence with its noble dome is justly regarded as a link between Gothic and Renaissance.

Lombardy and Tuscany, however, also have notable examples—most famed at Ferrara, Lucca and Pisa—of the peculiarly Italian method of decorating exteriors with tier upon tier of blind arcading and loggias which are such an enjoyable feature of Italian Romanesque architecture.

Rome, as one would expect, not only includes some of the earliest examples of Christian architecture but also some of the grandest. Even St. Peter's, however, is not a cathedral but a papal basilica, as are St. Paul's and S. Maria Maggiore, the cathedral of Rome being St. John Lateran. The most exotic and one of the best-known of Italian episcopal seats, St. Mark's, Venice, did not become one until 1807.

Features which make the Pisan group of ecclesiastical buildings one of the most memorable in the world are the leaning tower (or campanile) and baptistery. Campaniles and baptisteries, either detached or integral with the main fabric, are characteristic of Italian cathedrals, the former reaching heights up to 76 m (250 ft) and conspicuous in many northern cities, the latter much larger than is usual elsewhere because instruction was given in these buildings to catechumens before baptism and the sacrament itself was normally administered by the bishop in his own cathedral and even then only three times a year at Easter, Whitsun and Epiphany.

Internally, emphasis is more on length than height, often with no triforium. Many of the roofs are of wood and the arcades reflect the classical ideas on proportion and careful balance of mass and line with unmoulded square-ended arches and an air of solidity originating from ancient Rome. In the earlier basilican phases, such forms came in from the east across the sea (Byzantium) rather than over the more formidable barrier of the Alps.

The choir or presbytery of English cathedrals is sometimes separated from the nave by a pulpitum or stone screen, whilst in Spain the choir is completely enclosed and invisible from the congregation. This is not the practice in Italy but instead the presbytery is often raised above a large crypt, containing important relics or, possibly, the shrine of a saint to which pilgrims can pay their respects through a *confessio* or opening, to make it visible from the nave or from an ambulatory, entered from the aisles. The steps leading from the nave to the raised altar or down to the crypt make an equally effective division between nave and choir.

Although Italy is fortunate in possessing beautiful marble, good building stone is only found in the foothills of the Alps, Apulia and Sicily. Most of the cathedrals—and also St. Peter's—are basically of brick but full advantage was taken of the plentiful supply of columns and other material lying around amongst the ruins of ancient Rome and, at Syracuse in Sicily, the cathedral was formed out of the Greek Temple of Athena (built about 480 BC). It was by no means uncommon for pagan sites to be used in Italy, as elsewhere, for Christian purposes.

The fragmentation of Italy after the collapse of the Roman Empire tended to foster local styles and traditions, so that a Sicilian church was and still is utterly different in character from Roman, Tuscan and Lombardic examples. The country can be conveniently divided into areas for purposes of identifying these differences.

VENETO/RAVENNA (Aquileia, Grado, Torcello, Venice)

This area is unique in Italy in that, after being the last outpost of the Western Roman Empire before being submerged under the Goths, it was reconquered by Justinian for the Eastern Empire until the Byzantines were eventually expelled by the Lombards in 751. Both the Goths under Theodoric and the Byzantines under Justinian were enthusiastic builders of churches and it is to these influences that we owe the precious survivals in Ravenna with their magnificent mosaic work. The cathedral of Ravenna was, however, destroyed in the eighteenth century and the finest example in an episcopal building of the local style—basilican with timber roofs and much mosaic, stucco and inlay decoration with curious basket-work capitals—is now outside the country at Parenzo (Porêc) in Yugoslavia.

Aquileia and Grado. These neighbouring cathedrals demonstrate the typical basilican form. The former was a Roman colony and the original Christian church goes back to the beginning of official Christianity i.e. early fourth century; the bishop moved to Grado when Aquileia became too hot politically to stay in but both became episcopal sees when, at the end of the seventh century, the rivalry between them induced the Pope to give them equal status. Grado today is rather a run-down little building but Aquileia, although mainly of the eleventh century, is an outstanding episcopal church. Both are unique in having early mosaic pavements; the one at Aquileia, which covers both nave and aisles, is the most remarkable survival from the original early fourth century building, nowhere else to be found in such a well-preserved state, although only uncovered in this century.

Torcello. Originally built in 639, in the Venetian lagoons, this is another example of the local style. The present building is a reconstruction carried out at the beginning of the eleventh century with a campanile. In front of the choir is an iconostasis with saints painted as icons, further evidence of Byzantine influence.

Venice. St. Mark's (S. Pietro di Castello being the bishop's church before the nineteenth century) was probably originally in the same basilican style but the rise of Venetian power dictated something worthier of the city's patron saint and of the chapel of the Doges, and in 1603 a new building was started. The links between the great maritime power and Constantinople turned the builders towards Byzantine churches for models and as a result an entirely different design, used at San Sophia, in Greek cross form appears to have been followed, with five cupolas and colonnades around the arms of the cross. These cupolas rest directly upon the piers and there is no drum or lantern between; this developed later in Lombardy and spread from there elsewhere.

St. Mark's is adorned with lavish sculpture in stone and mosaic decoration which, over the Porta di S. Alipio, depicts the translation of St. Mark's body into the new church in 1094. The exuberance of it all makes this church a symbol of opulence and of the power of the Venetian Republic but much of the interior effect is lost by poor lighting. The effect externally when viewed from the Piazza di San Marco, however, together with the 98 m (323 ft) high campanile (rebuilt after collapse in 1902) is one of exotic splendour.

LOMBARDY and EMILIA/ROMAGNA (Como, Genoa, Milan, Modena, Parma, Pavia, Turin)

These provinces provide a link between the early Byzantine style of the Ravennate and the later development of mediaeval design in the northern half of the country. The new Romanesque style is seen in its purest Lombard form at Sant' Ambrogio in Milan (not a cathedral but founded by Bishop Ambrose at the end of the fourth century, rebuilt in the eighth and ninth centuries, and restored in the early part of the twelfth century).

Como. This is an example of the form which Gothic took in Italy before it was influenced by the designs used north of the Alps but, as we have seen, this style of architecture only took a very shallow root in the country and even at Milan (one of the largest churches in Christendom) the Lombard emphasis on proportion dilutes the essential Gothic lines.

Genoa. San Lorenzo, in Liguria, of mixed parentage, leads into the banded black and white marble which is found in Tuscany and Umbria. This is used on the façade (all that survived from a fire in 1296), and above the arcades of the French Gothic nave with Classical columns and blind triforium above.

Milan. Begun at the end of the fourteenth century, Milan took five hundred years to complete, even Napoleon taking a hand. Work on the 120 m (350 ft) spire was not started until 1750. This grandiose building made of marble with its forest of pinnacles hides a brick core and the vast and austere interior belies the splendour of the exterior. It is a monument to civic pride to which all classes contributed and the east windows of about 1390 are the largest in Europe.

Modena and Parma. Among diocesan churches, Lombard Romanesque is seen to best advantage at Modena and Parma. The Italian version is shorter than that found in England but with broader vistas and more elaborately decorated. Modena is consistent in style but the original wooden roof was changed to Gothic vaulting in the thirteenth century. The sculpture on the west front and on the capitals dates from the twelfth century and is from the hand of a famous carver of the time— Wiligelmo. The elevation of the presbytery is especially marked at Parma. Externally, the predominant motifs of these cathedrals are the blind arcading and loggias, used to great effect on the façade at Ferrara and probably derived from Pisa. Both Modena and Parma have striking campaniles, the former begun in the thirteenth century and completed with spire and lantern in 1319, the latter dating from c. 1290. The octagonal Romanesque baptistery at Parma is remarkable outside for having four tiers of open loggias and inside for the Veronese red marble used to face the walls. It is richly sculptured and painted throughout.

Pavia. Another late building started on an ambitious scale at the end of the fifteenth century, this was not finished until the present century in a modified reduced form with an interior entirely faced in marble. The dome, which is the third largest in Italy, dates from the end of the nineteenth century.

Turin. In Piedmont to the west, the cathedral, completed in 1497, has a pleasing exterior dwarfed by a large campanile erected in 1469 and rebuilt in 1720. It is famed for its Holy Shroud which was transferred in 1694 to a specially erected chapel.

TUSCANY/UMBRIA (Assisi, Florence, Lucca, Orvieto Pisa, Pistoia, Siena, Spoleto)

This heartland of Italy, where the Estes and the Medicis lorded it in the Middle Ages, and which was the wealthiest part of the country, naturally has imposing cathedrals but the greatest treasures architecturally date from the beginning of the mediaeval period. **Pisa**, started in 1063 after a great naval victory over the Saracens and consecrated in 1118, together with the baptistery, the leaning tower and the Camposanto is justly regarded as one of the great architectural thrills of the world; **Lucca** and **Pistoia** are delightful examples of the same style with open loggias and blind arches the source of which could have been Armenia and which had great influence elsewhere in Italy.

The interior of **Pisa** is distinguished by many of the columns being of granite with fine Corinthian capitals and bases taken from Classical ruins, and the use of banded stone foreshadows a practice which became widespread in Tuscany. The baptistery and leaning tower are too well-known to require description but attention should be given to the baptistery pulpit by Nicolo Pisano of 1260 which is regarded as the first great work of Gothic art in Italy and the beginning of Renaissance sculpture. Another fine pulpit by Giovanni Pisano (Nicolo's son) dating from between 1302 and 1310 is to be seen in the cathedral.

The later mediaeval episcopal churches (**Florence**, **Orvieto** and **Siena**), whilst impressive by their size or position and, in the case of Florence, by Brunelleschi's magnificent dome which overcame the problem of spanning a large central area and heralded some of the achievements of the Renaissance, show unmistakable signs of pride, and much of the decoration at **Siena** and **Orvieto** is what might be described as having the sweetness of confectionery. Nevertheless, the slender thirteenth-century campanile and cupola, and the interior of Siena with its outstanding paving, its harmonious lines and banded clustered marble piers are very impressive. The famous façade at **Orvieto** is in the form of a huge triptych. Giotto's campanile at **Florence** evokes mixed reactions and the interior of the duomo is gaunt and austere. Some of the greatest artists of the time were employed but one has a feeling that there were too many cooks. Nothing, however, can deny the dominance of the red, white and green marble exterior, the red roofs and inspired dome and lantern over the great city of Florence. The church is the second largest in Italy after St. Peter's basilica.

Two early mediaeval Umbrian diocesan churches of charm are S. Maria Maggiore at **Assisi** and the Cathedral of the Assumption at **Spoleto**. The portico at **Spoleto** is later and the belfry was added to the campanile in 1461.

LATIUM (Rome)

Rome. This city arouses thoughts of St. Peter's, the largest church in Christendom, the product of some of the greatest artists of the Renaissance—but mainly Michelangelo. Unfortunately, the time it took to build (nearly two hundred years) meant that others completed it and the effect at which Michelangelo aimed and his noble dome were marred by lengthening the nave and by the uninspired seventeenth-century façade which masks the dome. The interior, however, is most impressive and focuses on the amazing bronze baldacchino of Bernini which rises above the central altar.

The cathedral of Rome and the oldest in Italy going back to 320 is St. John Lateran, the very name of which recalls an old Roman family who owned the palace where the church now stands. It has, however, suffered over the years, being much altered in the seventeenth and eighteenth centuries, also burnt and neglected. The outstanding mosaic and marble floor was laid in 1425 but the most interesting feature is the cloisters which were added in the 1220s with coupled pairs of colonettes standing on a high plinth wall. St. John's claims to possess the head of both St. Peter and St. Paul. Only the Pope may celebrate Mass at the high altar.

The other papal basilicas are St. Paul's outside the Walls and S. Maria Maggiore—one of the earliest and largest churches dedicated to the Virgin Mary. St. Paul's was rebuilt in 1823 after being completely destroyed by fire but S. Maria Maggiore retains its main structure of the fourth century and much of the mosaic decoration from that time.

CAMPANIA (Amalfi, Naples, Ravello, Salerno)

Although a large part of Italy came under Spanish dominion in 1559, to be transferred in 1713 to Austria, the southern part of the country lost its independence long before that and as early as 1077 the Normans established themselves in Salerno, later to be succeeded by the French Angevins. In consequence this part of Italy with its beautiful coastal road round Amalfi and Salerno south of Naples shows a more pronounced foreign influence than further north, first Norman then Angevin importing the French Gothic style. It is also an area which has been subject to frequent devastating earthquakes, necessitating rebuilding and the consequent fusing of later styles on to the basic Romanesque.

Amalfi. Of the three cathedrals in the delightful area called the Salernitano, the one at Amalfi, which at one time was an important maritime power until it was sacked by Pisa in 1135, is of especial interest. The view of St. Andrew's Cathedral, hemmed in by houses and steep cliffs behind with the sea as a foreground, raised high up over streets tunnelled below, is a fascinating scene. The colourful polychrome façade is a nineteenth-century construction but the campanile is twelfth-century. The dedication reminds us that the relics of St. Andrew rest here.

Naples. Santa Maria Assunta Cathedral, destroyed by earthquake in 1456, was originally begun by Charles of Anjou in 1294. It was annexed to an earlier church (Santa Restituta) which goes back to Constantine's time. Santa Maria is famed for the miracles of the liquefying of the blood of San Gennaro (a martyr beheaded in 305). The crypt or Carafa Chapel contains the finest Renaissance work in the city.

Ravello. This cathedral has two fine pulpits and, like Salerno, handsome bronze doors (1266). One of the pulpit mosaic decorations tells the story of *Jonah and the Whale* and is of fine quality. The pulpits date from the twelfth/thirteenth century. The campanile is thirteenth-century.

Salerno. This building, which has suffered drastic restorations, is preceded by an attractive twelfth-century atrium and has a Romanesque bell-tower. It retains most of its early furnishings, including fine mosaic-decorated twelfth-century pulpits or ambos. It, too, retains the remains of a saint, in this case the evangelist Matthew. The bronze portal, reputed to have been made in Constantinople, dates from 1099.

125

APULIA

This little known heel of Italy is one of the most fruitful areas for the seeker of cathedrals for, under Frederick II, a crop of fascinating and highly individual diocesan churches grew up, ranging in style from the local Romanesque buildings of the north of the province, surprisingly influenced by Pisan styles, to the elegant Baroque creations of the south.

Amidst such abundance, one can only mention names and a few features.

Bari, as the principal city of the province, has a large and fine mother church (San Sabino) originally Byzantine, reconstructed in 1170 after an earthquake and recently restored. The south transept is particularly fine. Charming cathedrals from the Norman period are to be seen at **Troia**, **Barletta**, **Trani**, **Molfetta**, **Bitonto** and **Gravina** all grouped round Emperor Frederick's favourite residence at Castel del Monte.

Trani, built late eleventh/thirteenth century, of a honey-coloured stone, is, to quote Jasper More, 'one of the earliest, most elegant and most beautifully situated in Apulia' near the sea-front with its harbour. It has a large and graceful campanile and the crypt is even earlier than the rest of the building. **Barletta** reflects other styles, being partly fourteenth-century French Gothic and partly Renaissance, the former becoming influential when the Anjou family took over from the Norman rulers; the bell-tower is thirteenth-century. **Molfetta** of the twelfth/thirteenth century with three cupolas and twin western campaniles has been succeeded by a seventeenth-century cathedral. Two churches showing unmistakable signs of Pisan influence are **Foggia**, although rebuilt in Baroque style, and **Troia**, noted for its bronze door of 1127 and its pulpit. Both **Bari** and **Troia** are distinguished by jolly sculpture, animal heads used as corbels (cf. Kilpeck in Herefordshire, England) and, at **Bari**, special Apulian carving on the apse window. The fine Romanesque interior at **Troia** makes use of Classical columns.

Norman architecture reached its peak at **Bitonto**, which has a splendid façade with a large rose-window and fine sculptured doorways. Inside, this church has a good ambo, pulpit and crypt with thirty columns. A notable rose-window is to be seen at **Altamura** which, owing to rebuilding after an earthquake, combines Romanesque, Gothic and Renaissance features but in a most harmonious blend; the entrance doorway is outstanding with perhaps the finest Norman stone-carving in Apulia.

Baroque is encountered at **Martina Franca** but the local flowering of this style is seen to perfection at **Lecce** where full advantage was taken of a beautiful golden limestone, soft on extraction but hard after exposure—a perfect gift to an architect. The square is a joy with its fountain and many beautiful buildings. **Ostuni** has an attractive early fifteenth-century Gothic episcopal church and **Otranto** an eleventh-century example with an unusual mosaic floor.

So, Apulia's brief period of glory has left a legacy of highly individual Romanesque cathedrals with sculpture showing Saracenic and Byzantine influences.

To conclude, this fascinating region has in the cathedral of **Lucera** the most complete example of the Angevin style in southern Italy made of brick and stone, a rare instance of Gothic in the area.

CALABRIA (Tropea)

Tropea. A Norman Romanesque building on the edge of the ramparts dating from the eleventh century, it was rebuilt in the sixteenth century and restored to its original form in 1928.

SICILY (Cefalù, Monreale, Noto, Palermo, Syracuse)

Sicily, like Apulia, looks back to a more glorious past and despite severe earthquakes and the violence to which it has been subjected, we are fortunate in being able to enjoy the architectural heritage of those times. **Palermo, Monreale, Cefalù** and **Syracuse** are impressive buildings which include some of the finest mosaic decoration the world has ever seen. The oldest is **Syracuse**, a converted Temple to Athena, whose nave occupies the position of the temple *cella* (main rectangular chamber) with the original Doric columns still visible in the aisles. It has a fine Baroque façade. The church was severely damaged by earthquakes in the seventeenth/eighteenth centuries. **Palermo** is the largest of all royal Norman buildings in Sicily erected in the twelfth to fourteenth centuries but with the interior completely remodelled at the end of the eighteenth century. The royal tombs are of red porphyry, a very hard material which requires great skill to work.

The *pièces de résistance* are **Cefalù** and **Monreale** on the north side of the Island, founded in 1131 and 1174 respectively by the Norman kings Roger II and William II. Both have fine façades with twin symmetrical towers. **Cefalù** is smaller but the commanding apse in the dome of the presbytery is perhaps finer and it has a superb setting. The interior of **Monreale** with its inlaid marble floor of Arabic design, its walls covered by magnificent mosaics, lofty pointed arches resting on a complete set of granite columns, and capitals probably from a single ancient classical building, is unforgettable. Outside are delightful cloisters with richly and variously carved double capitals on twin columns of different shapes and decoration; a charming Moorish fountain in one corner completes the delight of this masterpiece of mediaeval art.

One cannot leave Sicily with its earthquakes without recording how, after the total destruction in 1693 of **Noto** by such a cataclysm, a free hand was given to the builder to reconstruct in Baroque resulting in a complete town in this style, including an imposing cathedral—another of Italy's great architectural delights.

SARDINIA (Cagliari, Sassari)

There are two diocesan churches.

Cagliari. Built in Pisan transitional Romanesque/Gothic style of the thirteenth century, this was remodelled in the seventeenth century. The fine pulpits came from the rood-screen of Pisa in 1162.

Sassari. This building, of many styles, was originally thirteenth-century but was remodelled in the fifteenth/sixteenth century. The campanile has a seventeenth-century crown. It has a Gothic interior and unusual Spanish Baroque façade of 1650–1723.

6
Russia

The study of Russian architecture can be said to begin with the acceptance of Christianity by Grand Prince Vladimir of Kiev in 988, after his
envoys had returned from exploring the merits of different religions.
Bedazzled by the splendour of the ceremonial they had seen in Greece,
which was so much in sympathy with the Russian love of colour, sound
and movement, they had strongly recommended the adoption of the
Greek faith. Vladimir married Anne, the sister of the Byzantine Emperor,
as a condition of his acceptance.

Close links were thus established with Byzantium and its style of architecture; this largely determined the course of Russian church design
and colourful decoration, with emphasis on mosaics and frescoes, until
the reign of Peter the Great (1689–1725). Western influences, however,
were not excluded, as evidenced by the carved relief sculpture, absence
of mosaics and simplicity of the white stone Cathedral of St. Dmitry,
dating from 1194–7, at Vladimir which became the capital of Russia in
1169.

During the period of Mongol invasion and domination which lasted
for two hundred and fifty years from the first half of the thirteenth
until the end of the fifteenth century, Russia was almost entirely cut off
from the West and only Novgorod of the larger cities managed, due to
geographical factors and astute dealings with the Tartars, to remain
independent, although acknowledging their overlordship and paying
tribute to them. Here, a more austere form of architecture developed
with steeper roofs and narrower windows suited to the severe climate
of the north.

In the meantime, building had to be in wood and the main outlet for
the Russians' artistic skills was the painting of icons, a skill which they
had learned from Byzantium. These were small enough to be possessed
and protected by every householder in this deeply religious land.

After Ivan III (1462–1505) had thrown off the Tartar yoke, Byzantine
influence continued because the Russians had been unable to keep
abreast of architectural developments elsewhere in Europe. Moreover,
Ivan's wife—who took the name Sophia—was the niece of the last
Byzantine emperor before the fall of Constantinople (Byzantium) in

1453, and Ivan himself took the emperor's title of *Caesar*, which became *Czar*. He embarked upon a major building programme based upon the style in use before the invasion and employing Italian architects as necessary. The churches were rectangular with apses—the most important external feature of Russian churches—rising to the cornices and domes which rested directly upon the roofs. Decorative motifs, however, became more colourful and the use of wood for building affected the design of arches and domes. This also encouraged the evolution of the half-spherical or helmet dome into the complete sphere with bulging sides on a lengthening drum, the typical onion dome so characteristic of Russia. Other features were the steeply roofed tent-shaped churches, the trapeza or gallery with open sides and the *kokoshnik* gable (so named after the curved and winged headdress worn by peasant women), all admirably suited to the severe climate for affording protection and throwing off snow.

Peter the Great's strong westernising influence was exercised more in the secular field than in churches and from the eighteenth century onwards, few ecclesiastical buildings of architectural note were erected except for the St. Petersburg cathedrals. The nineteenth century saw the same insensitive copying of the mediaeval as in England and this is reflected in the tasteless, over-ornate interior of St. Isaac's in Leningrad, completed in 1858.

The general design of Russian cathedrals is rectangular, having one or more domes and concentrating on internal decoration of frescoes and mosaics in the Byzantine manner. This responds to the Russian love of colour which is also reflected in the gilding and gay lines of the domes. The iconostasis creates a closed sanctuary effectively blocking off the priest from the congregation.

The designation 'cathedral' is applied somewhat indiscriminately to the chief church of a city which may at one time have been episcopal so that it is impracticable to describe them individually. Brief notes on some of them follow.

Kiev. The Monastery of the Caves, founded in 1051 by monks Anthony and Theodosius, comprises many cathedrals, other churches and monuments. There are fine murals in St. Michael's Cathedral (1070–88) in the surviving western part of the monastery. The twenty-one-domed and nine-aisled St. Sophia's Cathedral (now a museum) is the oldest in the country having been dedicated by Prince Yaroslav the Wise, son of Vladimir, in 1037. The 78 m (256 ft) bell-tower was erected in 1744–1852. There are interesting mosaics and frescoes in the central part and on the main dome and a marble tomb of Yaroslav, who was buried in

1854. There is also the nineteenth-century Vladimir Cathedral with seven gilded domes.

Leningrad. There are five cathedrals: the Cathedral of Our Lady of Kazan, the Cathedral of SS Peter and Paul in the fortress with a light and slender spire where all but one of the czars, from Peter the Great onwards, are buried in tombs of surprising simplicity, the huge St. Isaac's Cathedral built of granite and marble with a large gilded dome and a 68 m (223 ft) long iconostasis, St. Nicholas' Naval Cathedral, a functioning Orthodox church built in 1762 in Baroque style, and the Convent Cathedral of Smolny adjoining the former Institute for daughters of the nobility.

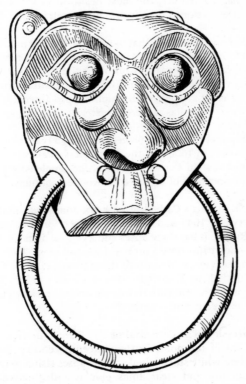

Doorknocker, Rostov, Russia.

Moscow. Of the four Kremlin cathedrals, the Cathedral of the Dormition (Assumption) with its five gilded domes, built in 1467–79 by Aristotele Fioravanti, an Italian architect, is the largest. From the fifteenth century onwards, the czars were crowned here. The Cathedral of the Annunciation with its nine cupolas (six were added later) was erected in 1482–90 by masons from Pskov and the Cathedral of the Archangel Michael in 1505–09 by another Italian architect, Alevisio Novi, in a style in marked contrast with the austerity of the other two cathedrals. Together with an earlier church on the site it was the burial place of Russian rulers (the likeness of the Russian princes and czars buried in it are painted on the walls of the forty-six tombs) until the reign of Peter the Great. The fourth Kremlin cathedral is the Cathedral of the Twelve Apostles built in 1655–56 which served as the Patriarch's private church. It is now a museum. Perhaps, however, the most beautiful in the Kremlin is the Church of the Deposition of the Virgin's Robe built in 1484–86 by Pskov masons.

The best known cathedral is that of Basil the Blessed in Red Square. It was built in 1555–60 by Ivan IV ('The Terrible'), to celebrate his capture of the Mongol capital of Kazan. A bizarre building, it is a combination of nine smaller churches—the 33 m (107 ft) high central structure being surrounded by eight chapels with onion-capped towers linked by an elevated gallery. Each has different exterior decoration, creating a Disney-like effect.

In Parade Square, there is the 98 m (320 ft) high Ivan bell-tower, built by Boris Godunov, in 1600 and the Granovitaya Palace.

In the Novodyevichi Convent there is the Smolensky Cathedral of 1525 with an iconostasis of eighty-four wooden columns.

Novgorod. St. Sophia's Cathedral with six domes was built by Greek architects between 1045 and 1062 and is therefore one of the oldest churches in Russia. It has three apses and a central dome in the shape of a soldier's helmet, capped by a bronze dove and cross. The Cathedral of St. George in the Yuriev Monastery dates from 1119–30. The steeply-gabled Cathedral of the Transfiguration was built in 1374. The Apparition of the Cross Cathedral with five onion domes and a brick balustrade on its façade is seventeenth-century.

Pereslavl-Zalessky. The Cathedral of the Transfiguration, apart from the replacement of the dome in the sixteenth century, goes back to 1152–58. Its fine white stone, single dome, apses rising to the height of the main structure and clean lines give it a distinctive, evocative appearance.

Suzdal. The town of Suzdal in the Vladimir region has been declared a national preserve on account of the wealth of its monuments. The most important are the thirteenth-century Cathedral of the Nativity with its five starred domes and, dominating the Suzdal Kremlin, the seventeenth century Monastery of St. Euphimi with its Cathedral of The Transfiguration dating from 1389, the Monastery of The Intercession with its three-domed cathedral and the Church of the Annunciation. The Pokrovsky Cathedral was the burial place of exiled czarinas.

Vladimir. The Cathedral of the Assumption, originally built as a single-domed church in 1158–61, was enlarged after a fire and given another four domes in 1185–89. The finest cathedral and one of the most outstanding in the country is St. Dmitry (1194–97). The exceptionally interesting sculptural decoration of the west front includes subjects from the Scriptures and Classical history; Solomon and Alexander the Great, for instance, are both represented.

Zagorsk. The Cathedral of the Assumption was built in 1585. Its five enormous bulb-shaped domes in blue and gold picked out with stars add to the vivid richness of the Trinity-Sergius Monastery's architecture, which includes the white Trinity Church with its beautiful helmet dome.

7
Spain (including Balearic Islands)

Of all the major architectural countries of Europe, Spain is the most highly individual, being the meeting-ground of two entirely different cultures, the Christian and the Moslem.

At the beginning of the eighth century, Islamic forces swept over the country from North Africa penetrating even into France until they were halted in 732 at Poitiers by the Frankish king, Charles Martel.

The subsequent history of Spain was the gradual process of reconquest—la Reconquista—and the effect on architecture was profound. In the meanwhile, the Moorish capital of Córdoba became the most civilised city in the western world and the channel through which Classical Greek culture was spread to Europe. Great tolerance was shown and Christians were allowed to practise their own religion, many of them using the Arabic language and developing their particular *mozárabe* art. Similarly, when Moslems came under Christian rule, another art form called *mudéjar* was evolved and these two forms are peculiar to Spain.

At first, Christian rule was confined to a small strip in the mountainous Asturias region of the north where, in about the year 718, a small band of determined men under their Visigothic leader, Pelayo, successfully repulsed a Moorish force sent to winkle them out of their cave fastness. This was the signal for a gradual extension of Christian rule along the north although the width of the area covered was not more than seventy-five, and in some places only twenty, miles. The fierce independence of the Basque part of the region is still evident today in the violence committed in the name of Basque autonomy.

As the crusade for the recovery of lost lands proceeded, the various divisions into which Spain was broken up slowly crystallised into the main provinces of Navarre, Castile and Aragon and, despite much internecine feuding, it was Castile and, to a lesser extent, Aragon, who spearheaded the reconquest, which culminated in the capture of Córdoba in 1236, Murcia in 1241 and Seville in 1248 and finally, after Ferdinand of Aragon had married Isabella of Castile, Granada in 1492. As each city was secured, new cathedrals were begun (Burgos in 1221, Toledo in 1226 and Palma de Mallorca in 1229).

The isolation of Spain and the difficulties of communication across its mountainous terrain made for conservatism in architecture and the Romanesque style brought in from France through the great march of pilgrims to the shrine of Santiago de Compostela, and from Lombardy to Catalonia through its trading connections, lasted over three hundred years. It was not until well into the thirteenth century that Gothic forms started to take its place. It may be that, with the development towards larger window areas, the change was delayed because this was thought unsuitable for the bright sunlight of Spain and cathedral interiors there are notoriously dark. But Gothic in its turn was slow to give way to later styles; Segovia and Salamanca were still being built with pointed arches during the sixteenth century.

Practically nothing remains in cathedrals from before the Moorish invasion and, in the southern part of the country, there is no Romanesque because it was under Moorish rule. The main examples are in the north where French influences were paramount except for the Lombardic impact on Catalonia. The Cluniac monastic order, which directed the pilgrim flow, naturally encouraged the art forms used in Burgundy although the south-west of France also made an impression. The French influence continued into the Gothic period and León, one of Spain's noblest cathedrals, is a smaller version of the great cathedrals of France but, as time went on, German, Flemish and, to some extent, English ideas were used as can be seen in the pinnacles of Burgos where Hans of Cologne worked and the lantern and spire of Toledo added by Hanequin de Egas from Belgium in 1448–52.

Sculpture and painting combined both idealistic and realistic elements. In the sixteenth century when Renaissance designs began to supplant Gothic, although often found together, Spanish bishops and nobles started to order their tombs from Italy, which was partly under Spanish rule, and the decoration of fruit, flowers, decorative panels and portrait medallions characteristic of Lombardic sculpture became fashionable. This developed into the Plateresque (from the Spanish for silver) style which, although used by silversmiths, was incorrectly ascribed to them. This elaborate appliqué art form, usually in square panels, is seen to best advantage in the university city of Salamanca and in its cathedral on the west front. Also peculiar to Spain is the later Churrigueresque of the eighteenth century, a name derived from several members of the Churriguera family who, working with another family named Quiñoñes, produced a wildly extravagant form best seen in the *Transparente* sculptured marble altarpiece of Toledo. They were architects, however, as well as sculptors but are best known for their huge gilt polychromed retables. Their work corresponded with the Baroque period of architecture and, although no completely new cathedrals were begun in Spain after 1600 except Cádiz and Lérida, many had new west fronts added in this style of which the outstanding examples are Murcia, Pamplona and Santiago de Compostela.

Spain is fortunate that during the nineteenth century there was no Gothic Revival and, so far as the present age is concerned, the unfinished church, although not a cathedral, of the Sagrada Familia at Barcelona by Antonio Gaudi, is a symbol that the creative spirit has not died.

The architectural forms evolved owe much to borrowings from abroad but, just as Roman, Visigothic and Moorish invaders were moulded by their environment so the architecture has been converted into something highly individual. Instead of the French emphasis on verticality and the English stress on length, Spain evolved a style aiming at large areas divided up into cubical blocks for chapels, sacristies, etc. and, externally, this massing has tended to obscure the form of the main structure with little indication that the designers were concerned overmuch with the exterior aspect of their work. The quality of the stone, however, especially that used at Salamanca and Segovia, often enhances the outside view.

Cathedrals were often erected on the sites of mosques and even of Classical temples (e.g. Seville, Tarragona and Valencia) and few face due east.

Despite the cathedrals being non-monastic, many have cloisters and chapter-houses. They were served by canons, not monks.

A typical and not very agreeable feature is the enclosing of the choir in what is called a *coro*, using part of the nave for this purpose, thus reducing the eastern extension and also diminishing the area available for congregations. It, moreover, takes away any through vista to the sanctuary.

Notwithstanding the political disunity caused by the Moslem invasions and the independent spirit of the people, Spain has remained a staunchly Roman Catholic country and, as a result, has been spared the fanatical vandalism of Puritans and Huguenots. Although suffering from a fratricidal and sanguinary Civil War from 1936–39, which fortunately resulted in relatively little structural damage to its main cathedrals, the country escaped the effects of the two Great Wars and has, therefore, preserved its mediaeval heritage of cathedrals, castles, palaces, even whole cities, better than any other Western European country, particularly the wealth of furnishings which have escaped the pillage and destruction of ardent reformers.

In view of the political disunity which prevailed during the Middle Ages and the stylistic differences which occurred in the different provinces, it is convenient to study the individual cathedrals regionally.

NAVARRE and THE BASQUE COUNTRY (Calahorra, Jaca, Logroño, Pamplona, Santo Domingo de la Calzada, Tudela)

This area, which has always been fiercely independent (the kingdom of Navarre was self-ruling from 905 until overrun by Castile in 1512), has one outstanding cathedral at **Pamplona**, a late Gothic building mainly dating from the first quarter of the fifteenth century but with a neo-Classical front of 1775–83. It is noticeably Spanish in its cubical proportions but gains greatly from the removal of the coro and the visitor is presented with a good example of harmonious design. The cloisters, built in two stages (early fourteenth and late fifteenth century), are among the finest Gothic examples in the country. Furnishings include the tomb of Charles III and his queen and a notable iron-work screen of 1517.

Jaca. An early example of the Romanesque style, dating mainly from 1054–63, it has been considerably altered. It also gains from the removal of its coro. There is a low massive tower at the west end. Features are the Plateresque portal in the Chapel of St. Michael and good twelfth-century wrought-iron screens.

Logroño. Santa Maria la Redonda, now a co-cathedral with **Calahorra**, is a fine example of the local type of hall-church built in 1480 to 1510 with a rotunda at the west end of 1742–60 and a Churrigueresque portal between the twin towers of 1769. The side chapels follow the Catalonian practice of being placed between internal buttresses. Both this cathedral and Calahorra, another late Gothic church, have star-vaults. The curious west front of the latter, with oblong tower, dates from 1680 to 1704 and is in a rather poor Baroque style; the Chapel of St. Peter has a fine fifteenth-century wrought-iron screen.

Santo Domingo de la Calzada. This dates from 1168 to 1235 with, on the south side, a detached eighteenth-century steeple which is comparable with some of Wren's best work in London and is one of the finest in Spain. The notable west door has seven orders. Furnishings include a Plateresque altarpiece of 1537–41, notable choir-stalls and bishop's throne of 1521–28, and many retables. Perhaps, however, Santo Domingo's best claim to fame is the chamber in the west wall of the south transept, closed by a grille, containing a live cock and hen, which are killed and replaced each 12 May in remembrance of a miracle in which a youth's innocence was proved by a roasted cock crowing on a table.

Tudela. This dates from 1194–1234 and is in transitional Romanesque/ Gothic style. It was founded as a collegiate church. One of the finest features is the west Puerta del Juicio richly sculptured with one hundred and sixteen separate scenes in its numerous orders depicting the *Last Judgement*. The charming Romanesque cloisters have interesting capitals, among the figures of which are miniature soldiers carrying pointed shields. Furnishings include a thirteenth-century sculptured Virgin and a handsome altarpiece of 1489–94.

OLD CASTILE and LEÓN (Astorga, Burgo de Osma, Burgos, León, Salamanca, Segovia, Zamora)

This heart of mediaeval Spain, which spearheaded la Reconquista, not unnaturally possesses fine cathedrals, notably Astorga, Burgo de Osma, Burgos, León and the new cathedral of Salamanca. León, built at the summit of Gothic achievement and retaining nearly all its original stained glass (but some restored), is outstanding among European cathedrals. The cathedrals in this region are, however, very varied, for whilst León is French, a German craftsman worked at Burgos, and Zamora is typically Spanish with its circular Romanesque central lantern, ribbed and covered with small stone fish scales.

León. Because of its outstanding importance, this must be taken first. This is a pearl among Gothic cathedrals, fit to rank with, but not as large as, some of the best French examples, dating from the second half of the thirteenth century. The south steeple with its open-work spire, however, was not completed until 1458–72.

The disciplined proportions of the interior and the abundance of original glass, ranging from the thirteenth century onwards, seen at its best in the rose-windows and the apse, make this cathedral a memorable experience.

The west front is also outstanding and the best of its kind in Spain, reminiscent of the recessed transeptal portals of Chartres and also, like them, richly sculptured. The towers are 65 m (213 ft) and 68 m (223 ft) high.

The coro enclosed by a carved and gilded alabaster screen dates from 1464.

Of furnishings, there are many episcopal and other tombs in the chapels which radiate from the ambulatory in French fashion and two tiers of 1467–81 stalls in the coro.

The fourteenth-century cloisters were altered in the sixteenth century.

Astorga. A late Gothic cathedral begun in 1431 (its nave completed in 1559), it is built of red and grey stone. It has a later Baroque west front of about 1700 with an unfinished northern tower. A peculiarity is the use of four-centred arches similar to those used in Tudor times in England. The fine retable was made by a pupil of Michelangelo and the well executed stalls date from 1551.

Burgo de Osma. A particularly good example of pure Early Gothic this was begun in 1232 and finished by 1300. Among many pleasures are the 72 m (236 ft) high Baroque tower, the stately south transept porch of c. 1300 with beautiful sixteenth-century statuary, cloisters (1500–23), splendid sanctuary screen (1505–15) and the main retable (1550–54). The tomb to S. Pedro de Osma in the north transept shows him in a natural attitude with his head upon a tilted pillow held by angels.

Burgos. The cathedral of the ancient capital of the province of Castile and León is on a larger scale than that of Burgo de Osma and contains many fine features, especially the magnificent 1482–94 Chapel of the Condestable at the east end. The exciting skyline of pinnacles and the 55 m (180 ft) high crossing lantern, dating from 1540 to 1568, add much distinction to the exterior.

The main fabric was started after the city had been reconquered in 1221 and was consecrated in 1260 but the west front, which has suffered from an insensitive eighteenth-century restoration, together with the towers, was not added until 1442–58.

The interior does not gain from unfortunate changes to the triforium and an unduly obtrusive coro. Below the lantern is a slab marking the tomb of El Cid and his wife.

Salamanca. This 'Oxford and Cambridge' of Spain has an old cathedral of the second half of the twelfth century with, alongside, a newer one of the first half of the sixteenth century. The older church is mainly Transitional in style; inside, its main feature is the dramatic upward vista into the two-tiered Romanesque central lantern. A notable early Renaissance fifteenth-century retable is to be seen in the apse.

The main attractions of the new cathedral, apart from the western tower, are the richness of the decoration, especially in the west doorway, and a particularly good coro dating from 1725–33. The western façade, built of a beautiful stone, is a handsome example of the Plateresque style which is such a feature of this city.

The two churches make a delightful prospect across the river Tormes.

Segovia. This is another cathedral with a striking exterior enhanced by its dominant position. It is also similar to the new cathedral of Salamanca in that it is a late Gothic building of the sixteenth century and is built of a lovely stone but it has a corona at the east end with chapels instead of the square east end of Salamanca. Segovia has a tall western tower 105 m (345 ft) high of 1620 and a dome over the crossing.

The beautiful cloisters of 1472–91 were moved from the old episcopal church in 1524.

Zamora. This Romanesque building of 1151–1224 has an impressive square western tower added a few years later and a fine central lantern with corner turrets and gables between. The cathedral gains greatly from its elevated site. The central lantern tower has an interesting ribbed dome divided into sixteen segments and this, together with the turrets and intervening gables, is covered with small stone fish scales.

The interior is characterised by the massive columns and the narrowness of the nave with castle-like capitals. The sanctuary dates from 1496–1506.

There are outstanding stalls, exceptionally fine screens and a good retable in the Chapel of the Cardinal (1466).

GALICIA and ASTURIAS (Oviedo, Palencia, Santiago de Compostela)

This area was situated on the great pilgrimage route to Santiago in the remote and somewhat melancholy lands of Galicia.

Oviedo. A fairly small building of fourteenth/fifteenth-century Gothic style, this is the only example in Spain to show French Flamboyant forms. The northern tower of the west front, dating from the beginning of the sixteenth century, was never finished but the southern tower, with an open-work spire, is outstanding and was completed with spirelets in 1556.

The cathedral is unusual in having pre-Conquest work in the much restored Cámara Santa of the ninth century, now used as a museum (the only other work of the period in Spanish cathedrals is at Palencia).

Palencia. This is a large fourteenth/fifteenth-century building in mature Gothic of good proportions. The nave (c. 1450–1516) is particularly distinguished by the purity of its lines. The crypt dates from about 673 and is therefore pre-Conquest.

Santiago de Compostela. This outstanding cathedral, which to the mediaeval pilgrim was second only in importance to Rome, is built of granite, which seems to reflect the character of the area.

Although the finest example of early Romanesque in Spanish cathedrals, anyone approaching from the west might be pardoned for thinking that they were in southern Germany for the view of the main façade at the top of a flight of steps brings one into the presence of exuberant Baroque.

The main fabric is late eleventh/early twelfth-century of great sobriety but the whole building was re-cased during the seventeenth/eighteenth century.

The outstanding piece of early work is the Portico de la Gloria (1168–88), a magnificent example of design and sculpture of the period. Inside, the interior is distinctive for the absence of a clerestory, its deep tribune storey and the massive austere simplicity of the long eleven-bay nave. Unusually for the period there is an ambulatory with radiating chapels to enable pilgrims to stop and pray at the shrine of St. James the Apostle whose body, in a marble coffin, was reputed to have been discovered by a Galician peasant in 813.

Later work includes the sixteenth-century cloisters, the belfry of 1676–80 beside the south transept and an octagonal lantern of 1384–1445.

CATALONIA and VALENCIA (Barcelona, Gerona, Lérida, Murcia, Tarragona, Tortosa, Urgel, Valencia)

Barcelona was concerned with commercial rather more than liturgical considerations and the effect on architecture was to encourage the building of hall-churches without aisles and the encompassing of the central area with chapels inserted between the internal buttresses, thus creating an unbroken exterior line. These broad internal spaces were suited to preaching to large congregations, as the friars, whose movement was strong in the area, liked to do, and the cathedrals were not unlike the main civic buildings.

Barcelona. The Cathedral was begun on 1 May 1298 and took about one hundred and fifty years to build but, although there were plans for it, the west front with its three open-work spires, which blends well with the rest, had to wait until the nineteenth century when a Barcelona industrialist came forward with the necessary funds; he was loyally succeeded by his son who gave the money for the dome, completed in 1913. The central spire rises from a fifteenth-century lantern.

On the north side is the fine door of St. Ivo in pure Gothic but the doorway to the charming cloisters of 1382–1448 is Romanesque.

The interior is somewhat severe with a raised altar. The chapels are continued right round the building as at Albi in France.

Decoration and furnishings are exceptional even for Spain with fine sixteenth-century marble reliefs on the coro screen depicting the *Life of Santa Eulalia*, the patron saint of Barcelona and a Diocletian martyr. Her shrine is in the crypt with a confessio for pilgrims. The pulpit, stalls and screen inside the choir are all expert work.

Gerona. Another fine Catalan hall-church of varying dates, it takes the place of an older church of which only the north (Charlemagne) tower and the cloisters (1180–1210) remain. It is one of the many Spanish cathedrals with a Baroque façade (1730–33); this is approached by a magnificent staircase. The earliest part is the chevet of 1312–47. The choir, together with its aisles, is no wider than the 22 m (73 ft) span vault of the nave. The fifteenth-century nave is surrounded by chapels. Furnishings include a splendid fourteenth-century altarpiece and canopy with panels depicting scenes from the Life of Christ. There is stained glass of the thirteenth and much of the fifteenth century. The tower dates from 1580–81.

Lérida. The old cathedral on the hill, now that it has been cleared and opened up after being a barracks for two hundred and fifty years, is an interesting example of the Transitional style (1203–78). The handsome octagonal belfry of 1391–1416, combined with the turret on the south transept and the lantern, make a pleasant exterior group. The church is preceded by cloisters (with curious capitals) like an atrium, entered through a fine late fourteenth-century portal—Puerta de los Apóstoles. There are remains of wall paintings of c. 1300 in the sanctuary. The new cathedral, gutted in 1936, has been restored.

142

Murcia. The cathedral of 1394–1465 was almost totally rebuilt in the eighteenth century after floods. It is distinguished by the work at the western and eastern extremities, the former a sumptuous example of Baroque (1736–54) and the latter a handsome apsidal chapel dating from c. 1495 to 1507. To the north is an impressive 90 m (295 ft) high tower, started in the sixteenth but not completed until the eighteenth century. The elegant Puerta de las Cadenas (chains) on the north side dates from 1512–15.

The western façade combined with the belfry makes a striking composition almost like a stage set. The eastern chapel (Chapel of the Vélez) is octagonal, decorated externally with large escutcheons and carved chains below, the badge of the Vélez family; inside, it has a beautiful screen and a notable polygon star-vault together with rich Plateresque decoration.

The interior of the cathedral suffers from a particularly obtrusive coro but is also adorned in the same style.

Tarragona. Conceived on a generous scale to serve an archbishopric covering a wide area, this was built on the site of a mosque, on which previously there had been a Roman temple to Jupiter. The dates being 1172 to 1289, the church provides an interesting example of the transition from Romanesque to Gothic.

Apart from the apse and the belfry, the exterior is lost in the surrounding buildings and the interior is dark and heavy but relieved by the delicate crisp carving of the capitals and bases of the piers and the later addition of a central lantern.

The notable doorway to the exceptionally fine cloisters of 1195–1215 has interesting sculpture. One capital in the east walk has a relief depicting the *Procesión de Las Ratas* in which a cat's funeral conducted by rats is interrupted by the awakening of the 'deceased'.

Tortosa. Although this cathedral was a long time being built (1347–1660), it is a consistent High Gothic church, apart from the Baroque front (1705–57), with one of the most beautiful ambulatories in Spain: double, with pierced stone screens having delicate tracery. Externally, the turrets on the flying buttresses and embattled parapets give a fortified appearance. There are appealing small cloisters on the south side.

Urgel. This appealing many-towered cathedral of 1131–82 set in a high valley by the tiny mountain community of Andorra is the work of a Lombard mason and shows typical blind arcading as well as an open gallery above the central apse. The cloisters have lost one walk and the transeptal towers are blind as if for defence.

Valencia. Built on the site of a Roman Temple of Diana, later used for a mosque, the cathedral was begun in 1262 and enlarged in 1480. Externally, it is distinguished by the Miguelete, an outstanding octagonal tower of Catalan style, and by its Baroque façade of 1703–13. The interior with very wide arcades and a central lantern was given a Classical look in 1774–79. In the handsome room of the old chapter-house (1356–69) there is an agate cup with golden handles and jewelled bands brought to the cathedral in 1437, claimed to be the Holy Grail. Undoubtedly of Roman origin, this treasure shows evidence of later alterations. The building was damaged by a mob in 1936.

BALEARIC ISLANDS (Palma de Mallorca, Minorca— Ciudadela and Ibiza)

Palma de Mallorca. With its magnificent site on the water front, this is one of the greatest and largest of Spanish cathedrals. It combines a masterful handling of internal proportions using tall, slender octagonal piers to support a vast space with effective exterior elevation, characterised on the south side by two tiers of irregularly spaced buttresses, with the noble porch of c. 1400 in the middle breaking their serried ranks.

Internally, although there is no triforium, the main vault at 42 m (141 ft) is higher than that of Amiens in France and with the tall aisles creates another hall-church. Basically fourteenth-century, the nave vaults, the springing points for which start from the main arcades, followed in the fifteenth century.

Minorca—Ciudadela. The parish church was raised to cathedral status in 1798. It is seemingly fourteenth-century but with a dome of 1615.

Ibiza. The hill-top site and slender spire of the church, which was made a cathedral in 1782, promise well but remodelling in 1712–28 has left an uninteresting interior except for the thirteenth-century sacristy with a good entrance. The rampart walls give a fortress-like appearance.

ARAGON (Huesca, Saragossa, Tarazona, Teruel)

This largely mountainous country with its capital at Saragossa was allied with Catalonia in the Middle Ages and together they acquired Valencia and the Balearic Islands by conquest from the Moors. Although little tolerance was shown towards Moslems their *mudéjar* art form was assimilated so that the architecture of Aragon has a distinctive regional flavour.

Huesca. This is a blend of an old cathedral begun in 1278 to which belongs the fine west portal of c. 1300–13 and a late Gothic structure of 1497–1515. The main feature of the interior, of which the aisles are well below the level of the nave, is a very richly sculptured altarpiece of 1520–34 showing, as the main theme, the road to Calvary, the Crucifixion and the Deposition, with numerous figures above and below in canopied niches.

Saragossa. This town is unusual in having two cathedrals, each enjoying the status of the seat of the archbishop and his chapter for six months of the year. The older—La Seo—was converted from a mosque in the eleventh century but was successively enlarged and is today mainly a structure of the mid-sixteenth century with a seventeenth-century façade. Externally, it is chiefly notable for its tall brick steeple of 1682–90 with bulbous cap, Plateresque decoration and the octagonal brick lantern of 1498–1520; other features are the north-eastern walls of a chapel and the apse made of panelled brick with inlaid glazed tiles. Inside, it is an imposing hall-church of five aisles with reticulated vaulting and a fine star-vault in the lantern. The capitals of the slender pillars are carved with figures of children. The alabaster retable in the sanctuary dates from 1431 to 1477.

The other cathedral—El Pilar—recalls the legendary appearance of the Virgin descending on a marble pillar to St. James the Great when he was preaching in the year 40. It is a vast building of exotic aspect having a central dome surrounded by smaller cupolas with coloured tile roofs and lanterns, and bulbous-capped towers in two corners (the others were not completed). It was started in 1677 but dates mainly from 1754–66. The interior is richly decorated.

Tarazona. The cathedral of this mountain town, built in 1152–1235, provides an interesting study of brickwork. This material is used in the impressive lantern by the designer (who erected the one at La Seo, in Saragossa), the gallery which runs round the top of the chevet, the south-west tower (*mudéjar* work) and the late Gothic cloisters of 1504–29 (the most attractive feature). The interior of 1500–88, disparate in style but with a good eastward vista and star-vaulting, is also of brick.

The Capilla (chapel) de Calvillos has notable Renaissance alabaster tombs.

Teruel. The main feature of the cathedral is the wooden painted coffered ceiling in the nave (called *artesonado* work) of c. 1260–1314. Basically of 1248–78, the church was altered later and, after becoming a cathedral in 1577, was much enlarged and provided with brick transepts. The western tower was started in 1257 and has a seventeenth century crown. There is a central octagonal brick lantern similar to those at Saragossa and Tarazona. The Plateresque retable is noteworthy.

NEW CASTILE and ESTREMADURA (Plasencia, Sigüenza and Toledo)

This is a land which has experienced a decrease in population. A dry and arid plateau, much of it is deserted or used mainly for pasture. The home of Cortes, conqueror of Mexico, and Pizarro, conqueror of Peru, it was from this region that many of the more adventurous Estremadurans went overseas because of limited opportunities in their native province. Castile, named from the many castles erected for defence against the Moors, includes the white, hot and windswept plains of La Mancha where Don Quixote had many of his adventures. Small windmills dot the landscape.

These provinces contain one major cathedral at Toledo and the outstanding eastern parts of a diocesan church at Plasencia.

Plasencia. In the Estremadura, this is the most exciting and architecturally the most outstanding. It combines a grand rebuilding of the eastern parts between 1498 and 1537 with the retention of the old cathedral nave and therefore is similar in this respect to Le Mans in France and Gloucester in England. The earlier cloisters of 1416–48 and the Transitional thirteenth-century chapter house with dome also remain. The main Renaissance portal on the north side dates from 1558.

The scale of the new part is breathtaking, wider than some of the largest European cathedrals with a span exceeding even that of Seville. It is a hall-church of sober lines covered with delicate intricate vaulting raised on unbroken shafts creating a canopy-like structure.

Furnishings include a noteworthy retable of 1626 and good carving on the choir stalls, of 1492–1520 with marquetry decoration.

Sigüenza. This is a powerful dominating building in which the exterior counts for as much if not more than the interior. With massive, castellated western towers flanking a broad perfectly plain façade with fine round-arched door, the outside looks severe. On the south side, the transept has a good rose-window and there is another tower next to the central lantern.

The interior is confused except for the south transept dating from 1155–69. The dates of the building in general are c. 1150 to 1495 and it is mainly French in derivation. The sixteenth-century sacristy is beautifully vaulted and decorated.

There is much to enjoy in the furnishings—good fifteenth-century stalls, splendid paintings in the Chapel of Santa Librada (an outstanding example of Renaissance work) and, above all, *El Doncel de Sigüenza*, a splendid sixteenth-century sculpture in the chapel of the Arce family showing the figure of Martin Vazquez de Arce who fell in the last stage of the campaign against the Moors in 1486 during the attack on Granada. The young knight is shown leaning on his elbow reading a book. The monument dates from c. 1495.

Toledo. This building can be counted amongst the major architectural achievements of the world, a worthy seat for the Primate of Spain.

With its emphasis on area and cubical massing, it is very Spanish as befits a city the whole of which has been declared a national monument. Both outside and in, it is outstandingly impressive, and the west front, dating from 1418–52, with its magnificent 90 m (295 ft) north-west tower (1380–1440), is a fine composition. The spire, added by a Belgian architect, Hanequin de Egas, in 1448–1452, is encircled with three bands of horizontal rays symbolising the Crown of Thorns.

The cathedral was started in 1227 and was completed in the main in 1493, although it embraces every style from the thirteenth to the eighteenth century. The dome (1631) of the south-west cupola was designed by the son of the painter El Greco.

The majestic interior is five-aisled; eighty-eight piers support the vault, all in a pure Gothic style. It is adorned with seven hundred and fifty stained glass windows dating from 1418 to 1560 and the furnishings are so numerous as to preclude listing. One should mention the huge sculptured Flamboyant larchwood retable of 1502–04 in the sanctuary, fine stalls of the fifteenth/sixteenth century and a number of paintings in the sacristy by El Greco, Goya, van Dyck and Titian. Behind the high altar is the extravagant Churrigueresque *Transparente* sculptured marble altarpiece (so-called because it is lit by a window cut through the vault above).

Sculptured marble altarpiece, Toledo, Spain.

ANDALUCIA (Cádiz, Córdoba, Granada, Jaén, Seville)

This romantic land was the last to be recovered from the Moors and, consequently, all the cathedrals are late buildings. With the predilection of the Andalucians for the exaggerated, the cult of the colossal is manifest in its cathedrals and they are nearly all very large, in the case of Seville the biggest mediaeval example in the world. There is much Renaissance work and no Romanesque.

Seville. In contrast to Córdoba, the conquering Spaniards pulled down the old mosque, except for the exquisite Giralda (94 m [309 ft] high, erected in 1184–98 with a Renaissance open belfry stage and crown of 1560–68), and built from scratch between 1402 and 1506 although retaining the ground plan of the mosque. Externally, the main impression is of great mass, numerous pinnacles and ornate mainly modern façades with no vertical emphasis from towers.

Internally, it is of enormous grandeur with double aisles and a vast area sustained on clustered piers with the minimum of support. The vault of the double-aisled nave is 37 m (121 ft) high and the length/width are in proportion. Of the many chapels, the most important is the Capilla Real of 1551–75.

Among the many furnishings, one may mention the Plateresque retable of 1482–1525 (wings 1550–64), which is one of the largest in Spain, in the sanctuary, the huge nineteenth-century monument to Christopher Columbus in the south transept and eight Murillo paintings in the sacristies and chapter-house.

The designers aimed at a church which, according to the minutes of their decision, would be 'so good that there shall be none its equal' and they certainly achieved this in regard to size. In addition, it has great harmony of style and excellence of proportion.

Cádiz. The cathedral, situated by the harbour, is another very large church but a striking contrast to Seville in being a Baroque building of 1722 to 1838, the only complete episcopal example of this style in Spain. The towers were completed in 1853.

The rotunda-shaped sanctuary is surmounted by a cupola and the apsidal transepts abut on to a central dome sheathed in glazed yellow tiles. The wide west front is marred by the later upper stage and the contrast of white stone used for this work with the older brown material.

The interior has a satisfying spaciousness with flowing curves and a choir with good stalls.

Córdoba. The city, known as *el horno* (oven) because of the heat in summer, affords one of Spain's strangest architectural sights—a late Gothic cathedral with Plateresque decoration set in the middle of a huge mosque, which measures nearly 183 m (600 ft) by 122 m (400 ft). The mosque is a vast building of nineteen naves with about eight hundred and fifty columns of marble, jasper, breccia and porphyry, mostly smooth but some with spiral decoration, averaging about 4 m (13 ft) in height, supporting double arcades with white stone and red brick voussoirs and affording delightful vistas. In the middle of this was planted an unworthy cathedral begun in 1523 and completed in 1598, except for the Renaissance oval dome, which was added in the following two years. The tower to the north is a Renaissance alteration of the minaret carried out from 1593 to 1617, with the lantern added in 1664 increasing its height to 93 m (306 ft). There is a handsome red marble retable surmounting the raised high altar and Churrigueresque stalls of 1747-58.

Granada. Another huge cathedral, this took nearly two hundred years to build (1523-1703). Although it has five aisles, it is uninspired and marred by a tall dome raised on stilts to take the place of an apse. The plain west front of 1667-1703 is heavy and cold but of good proportions. The interior gains from having no coro.

The main pleasure is the Capilla Real alongside (1506-21) in Gothic style with attractive vaulting. This beautiful building was designed as a mausoleum for Ferdinand and Isabella, and their daughter, Joan the Mad and her husband, Philip of Burgundy. The monuments are in white marble with fine effigies.

Jaén. The cathedral is a fine Renaissance structure, taking from 1540 to 1726 to erect. The noble west front, flanked by twin 62 m (203 ft) high towers dates from 1667 to 1688. The interior is a hall-church with vistas both lengthwise and upwards to the dome and the domical vaults. The excellent proportions and the quality of the work make this a building of exceptional grace. The walnut coro dates from c. 1500 to 1530.

8
Other European Countries

AUSTRIA

The lively Baroque form of art, which became so much part and parcel of the spirit of the Austrian people, is best seen in the cathedrals at **Salzburg** and **Linz** but the most famous of the country's episcopal churches, St. Stephen's at **Vienna**, is a Gothic hall-church dating from 1300–1510, distinguished externally by its splendid steeple, affectionately known as 'Alter Steefl' or 'Old Steeve', and its huge steep roof with patterned tiles.

Of other cathedrals the most interesting is **Gurk** in Carinthia, once, like Salzburg, the seat of prince-bishops, a twin-spired mainly Romanesque building with triple apses. **Klagenfurt**, also in Carinthia, dates from the sixteenth century. **Graz**, in Styria, is fifteenth-century Gothic, noted for its exterior fresco painted in 1498 depicting *Divine Torments* (plague, locusts and war).

DENMARK

The cathedrals of Denmark are much restored and show North German influence. None are of the first rank. The main building material is brick (Aarhus, Haderslev, Odense, parts of Ribe, and Roskilde, the country's most notable episcopal church).

Aarhus has the longest nave 92 m (303 ft) in Denmark whilst **Copenhagen** was rebuilt after bombardment by the British fleet under Admiral Nelson in 1807. **Odense**, founded in 1080, is considered one of the best examples of Gothic church architecture in the country. The interior is rendered entirely white.

Roskilde Cathedral has been a royal mausoleum since the fifteenth century and it is chiefly noted for the chapels and monuments to kings and queens, added as the need arose, and enabling one to follow the development of Danish architecture from the fifteenth to the nineteenth century. The interior is a contrast of red and white, the piers of brick and the rest stuccoed or plastered. There are elaborate furnishings.

EIRE

Witnesses to a troubled history, many cathedrals are roofless and others are largely, if not entirely, nineteenth century or later. Evidence of the disturbances is given by church towers resembling those of fortified castles (Christ Church and St. Patrick's, **Dublin**—both Protestant in this largely Roman Catholic city, St. Canice's at **Kilkenny** and St. Mary's at **Limerick**) whilst St. Brigid's at **Kildare** has a continuous embattled parapet.

There are many notable monuments, especially the huge five-storey seventeenth century one to the Boyle family at St. Patrick's, Dublin, the Renaissance example to Donogh O'Brien, Earl of Thormond, dating from 1678 at St. Mary's, Limerick, which also has a fine set of twenty-three choir stalls of 1480–1500, all, except three, with misericords, and the handsome mid-eighteenth-century tomb to Archbishop Cox and his wife at St. Canice's by the famous Belgian sculptor, Scheemakers.

Perhaps the outstanding nineteenth-century cathedral is St. Finbar's at **Cork**. St. Colman's at nearby **Cobh** with lofty tower and spire rises dramatically above the harbour.

FINLAND

In a land noted for the achievements of its modern architects, there is much in contemporary buildings to admire. The cathedral at **Helsinki**, dating from 1830–40, forms part of a group consisting of cathedral, university and senate building in Senate Square, all designed in neo-Classical Empire style by the German-born Carl Ludwig Engel; with its enormous cupola it is the city's most famous landmark.

Turku (called 'Abo' by Swedish-speaking Finns), the seat of the Primate of Finland, has an episcopal church over seven hundred years old but it has been twice gutted by fire, the second time in 1827, since when it has been completely restored.

GREECE

Athens' first cathedral was the Parthenon which was converted into a church in the sixth century. Later it became a mosque.

Subsequently, the tiny church known as Panagia Gorgoepikoos or Agios Elefterios measuring externally only 12 × 7.6 m (40 × 25 ft) and with a cupola under 12 m (40 ft) in height was the metropolitan church.

In its present form it dates from the twelfth century although legend attributes its foundation to the Empress Irene in c. 787. The present cathedral, built 1840–55, lies to the north of this diminutive building.

There is another cathedral—the Metropolitan Church of Agios Dimitrios—at **Mistra**, dating from 1309. The basilica was altered in the fifteenth century when the upper part was replaced by five domes. The arcade of the marble iconostasis has unusual fretwork carving.

MALTA

The main cathedral is at **Mdina** (the capital before Valletta was built), erected in Renaissance style after an earthquake in 1693.

The co-cathedral of St. John's at **Valletta**, consecrated in 1578, is austere without but sumptuously decorated within; on each side are chapels of the *langues* (national divisions) of the Order of the Knights of St. John.

The Anglican cathedral at Valletta owed its origin to the determination and money provided by the Dowager Queen Adelaide, widow of the English king, William IV. Built in neo-Classical style, it has an elegant font placed within a pillared cupola and an organ which came from Chester Cathedral. Off-set to the south side is a 61 m (200 ft) high spire. The church is built of the warm, golden-coloured limestone which is such a feature of Malta.

NETHERLANDS

The form of worship that emerged in the north of the Netherlands after the Reformation was not conducive to either the founding or the enrichment of cathedrals.

Utrecht was even more unfortunate in that, in 1674, a violent storm blew down its nave so that the massive 103 m (338 ft) high tower (1321–82) is separated from the rest of the church (choir and transepts) by an open space. Nevertheless the choir, rising to 35 m (115 ft), impresses by the excellent proportions of arcade, triforium and clerestory, even if the absence of decoration gives an austere and joyless effect.

St. John's at **s'Hertogenbosch**, in the mainly Roman Catholic province of North Brabant, affords a striking contrast, being a richly adorned Late Gothic edifice, rebuilt between the end of the fourteenth and beginning of the sixteenth century. The double-aisled and finely-proportioned nave in Flamboyant style rises to over 30.5 m (100 ft). A

St John's Cathedral, s'Hertogenbosch, Netherlands.

touch of fantasy is provided externally by the swarm of little stone manikins scrambling over the flying buttresses and up the steep copings to escape from the demons.

NORWAY

Norwegian cathedrals are strongly English-influenced and have square east ends rather than apsed ambulatories with radiating chapels as in France.

Of the six diocesan churches (Bergen, Kristiansand, Oslo, Stavanger, Trondheim and Tromsö), **Trondheim** is undoubtedly the outstanding building not only in Norway but in the whole of Scandinavia, although it has suffered grievously and is still in a state of reconstruction to the design originally planned for it. The mid-thirteenth-century nave is one of the best parts, modelled on the Angel Choir at Lincoln, but for five hundred years until 1930 it had no roof and the upper parts are new.

Stavanger combines a five-bay Norman nave with much spirited carving on the capitals with a Gothic choir (rebuilt after a fire in 1272). **Bergen** with a single western tower dates from the thirteenth/fourteenth century, **Oslo**, consecrated in 1697, was restored in 1849–50, **Kristiansund** was rebuilt in Gothic style after destruction by fire in 1880 and **Tromsö** completed in 1861, is one of the largest wooden churches in Norway.

PORTUGAL

Although Portugal's history followed similar lines to that of Spain, architecture nowhere reached the heights of Santiago, León and the other great Spanish cathedrals. During the golden age of exploration and discovery between 1480 and 1520, the extraordinary and exotic form of Manueline decoration (named after King Manuel I) held sway, a style peculiar to Portugal. Prior to this, and in the Early Gothic period, French influence predominated and the early bishops were often French. The best Romanesque work in cathedrals, but on a modest scale, is to be seen at Braga, Coimbra and Oporto. Gothic is most effectively represented in the great abbeys of Alcobaca and Batalha.

Azulejos, blue glazed ornamental tiles, used both externally and inside, are a particularly Portuguese form of adornment.

The cathedrals are often built on a high point in the centre of a city and some (Coimbra, Lisbon, Oporto) preserve their fortified appearance, resembling the castles with which their defences were combined.

Sculpture tends to concentrate on funerary monuments rather than on doorways, capitals, etc.

Evora, although only a modest building, is perhaps the best of Portugal's cathedrals. Built of granite in twelfth/thirteenth-century Transitional style, nave and transepts converge on a fine octagonal dome. The other architecturally interesting diocesan churches are **Braga** (remodelled internally in Baroque form and distinguished externally by a graceful statue under a Flamboyant canopy of the Virgin Feeding the Child—*Nossa Senhora do Leite*, **Coimbra** (built 1140-75 by French masons), **Guarda** (built of granite), **Lisbon** (end of twelfth century but severely damaged by the earthquake of 1 November 1755), **Oporto** and **Viseu**.

SWEDEN

Many of the cathedrals are formidably restored and are not of first rank but there is much variety and some notable work. They are all in the southern part of the country (**Visby** is on an island).

The cathedral of **Lund**, begun in about 1080, is the only substantial Romanesque church in this part of Europe. Mainly of grey sandstone, plus granite on the north side, it was thoroughly restored to its original state in 1833-78 following many fires and a long period of neglect after the Reformation. Below the interior is a large crypt with twenty-three pillars, two of which are adorned with figures of the legendary giant Finn and his wife. Lund was the coronation church of Swedish kings from 1528 to 1721.

The cathedral of **Uppsala**, Sweden's oldest university city, is the seat of the Archbishop. It is a French-inspired building but with the limitations imposed by the brick of which it is built. Western spires, completed in 1893, are 118.5 m (389 ft) high. The main structure took from 1287 to 1435 to erect. There are no triforia. It was restored in 1883-93.

Linköping, with a ten-bay nave which is the longest in Scandinavia and a single western spire 105 m (344 ft) high, is a hall-church which took even longer to build (1150 to 1498). The spire was completed in 1886.

Brick is the main material of **Stockholm** (a hall-church made diocesan in 1942), **Strängnäs** (consecrated in 1291 but not finished until the end of the fifteenth century, with a large western tower with Baroque crown and a Flemish reredos considered to be the finest in Scandinavia) and **Västerås** (attractive brick tower over 91 m [300 ft] high).

Chur Cathedral, Grisons district, Switzerland.

SWITZERLAND

Switzerland's dozen cathedrals range from the somewhat sombre interior of **Chur** (the capital of the Grisons region)—a building of only parish church proportions—to the Rococo exuberance of **St. Gallen**—but sobriety, as one would expect in the land of Calvin, is usually the keynote. French, German and Italian influences are all felt in this turntable of Europe. The cathedrals suffer from the German tendency towards over-restoration, with coloured and patterned diamond tiles, often a disturbing feature.

The setting is often attractive as one would expect in this beautiful land. Romanesque is not so strongly represented as in Germany.

The finest of the Gothic cathedrals and strongly French-influenced is **Lausanne** but it is much restored. The construction of **Fribourg** with its handsome fifteenth-century tower was spread over a long period from 1283 to the seventeenth century.

A late Gothic cathedral is **Berne**, started in 1421 and completed in 1573 but its tall single western tower with short open-work spire was not finished until 1873.

Post-Reformation examples include **Lucerne**, rebuilt in Renaissance style after a fire in 1633, except for the Gothic towers and **Lugano** which also displays Renaissance influence.

Many of the porches are of interest, especially the St. Gallus portal at **Basle** and there are many good choir stalls but the stained glass in general is not outstanding.

YUGOSLAVIA

In the Adriatic coastal regions of Istria and Dalmatia, which are formed of limestone, architecture and sculpture predominate. Further east, frescoes and icon-painting are the chief modes of artistic expression.

It has to be said, however, that, with the exception of **Sibenik**, **Zadar** and **Zagreb**, the cathedrals are not above parish church dimensions.

As in Italy, the Romanesque style of architecture lingered a long time and the west front of **Zadar** cathedral with its agreeable sculpture completed in 1324, ranks among the latest work of this style in Europe. On the other hand, the Renaissance style came in early so that Gothic had a relatively short innings. The typical Yugoslav Romanesque church is basilican with nave, aisles and an apsidal east end. **Krk**, **Kotor**, **Rab**, **Trogir** and **Zadar** are basically of this type and the only mainly Gothic cathedral is **Korčula**.

9
Modern Cathedrals

AUSTRALIA

Brisbane. Designed by the eminent Victorian architect, J. L. Pearson, and continued by his son, the foundation stone of Brisbane Cathedral was laid in May, 1901. The outer walls are of porphyry, a very hard stone, and the interior of local Helidon stone. Designed in fourteenth-century French Gothic style, the ambulatory and vaulting make a fine impression and it is much to be hoped that this notable building can one day be completed.

Melbourne. There are three spires on each of the two cathedrals (St. Paul's, Anglican—1880–91 and St. Patrick's, Roman Catholic—1858–97). These were added between 1921/1926 and 1937/39 respectively. The nave of St. Patrick's has a fine hammer-beam timber roof.

Adelaide. The cathedral at Adelaide, originally designed by the highly individual Victorian architect, William Butterfield, dominates the cricket ground, reminding one of Worcester in England.

BRITISH ISLES

Coventry. The present cathedral is an essay in contemporary style built in only six years between 1956 and 1962 to replace the parish church which had served as the mother church since 1918 when the see was created; this had been gutted, except for the 90 m (295 ft) tower and spire, by bombs in November 1940. The ruin of the old church is used as a forecourt and is linked with the new by a staircase descending to the lofty entrance porch.

Concessions were made to tradition by facing the exterior with red sandstone of good quality and the view from the south-west shows well the saw-tooth arrangement of the windows, which directs light onto the altar. The Epstein statue of *St. Michael and Lucifer* on the south wall is of bronze.

The interior, although only 82 m (270 ft) long is spacious and seemly with furnishings by many noted contemporary artists.

Guildford. Built mainly between 1952 and 1965 in traditional style, (but started before World War 2) this modern cathedral makes the most of its excellent hilltop site and has respected the limitations of the material used (bricks made from local clay) by not indulging in ornamentation and by good massing.

Inside, the brick is rendered with plaster and limestone is used for the dressings, creating an air of light and space, enhanced by the hall-church design of the nave. The narrow aisles provide interesting vistas. The furnishings, however, are unworthy.

Liverpool. The twentieth century is well represented by the two cathedrals at Liverpool, so different in styles, scale, atmosphere and the time which they took to erect. The Roman Catholic cathedral is bold in design, circular with a sense of coloured spaciousness within and took only five years to build (1962–67), but the steel and concrete of which it is constructed are unsympathetic. The building is supported by sixteen trusses, which splay out radially from the base of the tapering tower, and is completed by its famous corona of stainless steel. The whole of the tower between the struts is made of coloured glass.

The Anglican cathedral also gives a feeling of spaciousness inside and on a much larger scale but the effect, except at the crossing, is rather solemn. Externally the great massing of masonry, the enormous bulk and the noble 101 m (331 ft) high tower with its octagonal corona—the best feature—are impressive and give the cathedral a dominating position in the Liverpool townscape. It took seventy-four years to build, completion being marked by a Service of Thanksgiving and Dedication in the presence of the Queen on 25 October 1978.

KENYA

Nairobi. All Saints' Cathedral erected between 1917 and 1952, is unusual in that the towers and three bays of the nave were the first parts to be built (the towers are usually the last) and also because the towers are transeptal, as at Exeter in England, and are of the Scottish saddleback type. The material is granite and the cathedral is set above the city in attractive gardens.

NEW ZEALAND

Auckland. The foundation stone of the Cathedral of the Holy Trinity was not laid until June 1957 and building was not begun until 1959. Only one-third of the project has yet been completed, consisting of the eastern end built of reinforced concrete on piers sunk 10.5 m (35 ft) into the ground. The brick cladding makes it strikingly reminiscent of Guildford Cathedral in England. There remains to be constructed all the principal parts—choir, sanctuary, nave (to be a curious tent-like structure), baptistery and narthex. Galleries giving both interior and exterior views are also planned.

SOUTH AFRICA

Cape Town. St. George's Cathedral was begun in 1901 by Herbert Baker—architect, with Lutyens, of New Delhi—and replaced an earlier church. The latter, created a cathedral in 1848, bore a striking resemblance to St. Pancras' Church in London. Work has been interrupted more than once and the western part is yet to be constructed whilst, in the absence of a belfry, the eight bells still lie on the ground. The golden colour of the Table Mountain sandstone imparts a warm atmosphere to the choir and apsed sanctuary but perhaps the most arresting feature is the set of clerestory windows, designed by the outstanding French glass-maker, Gabriel Loire, who has his studio at Chartres (where better?), depicting in graphic colours the story of the Creation.

The cathedral possesses a very ancient Coptic cross discovered on a battlefield after the destruction of Magdala, Abyssinia, in 1868.

U.S.A.

New York (St. John the Divine). This, the largest cathedral in the world (although exceeded in surface area by Seville, Spain) was started in 1902 to a Romanesque-Byzantine design. When work was resumed in 1916, after an interval of five years, Gothic ideas prevailed so that we see at St. John the Divine a Romanesque choir linked to a Gothic nave through a temporary crossing. The overall length is 183 m (601 ft) and the height of the nave to the ridge rib 38 m (124 ft), loftier than the nave of any church in England and only exceeded by Amiens and Metz in France, Cologne in Germany and Palma de Mallorca in Spain.

The use of stone and tiles of varying colours in the choir, which is surrounded by seven radiating chapels in the French fashion each dedicated to one of the major ethnic groups in the city (the Chapels of Tongues) was inspired by the description of the New Jerusalem in the twenty-first chapter of the *Book of Revelation*. There is some notable stained glass, particularly that by Charles J. Connick. The nave was ready for use by 30 November 1941 but seven days later the Japanese struck at Pearl Harbour and work came to a grinding halt.

Now this cathedral, situated in a rather remote part of town, is to be restarted and, although the towers, crossing, transepts and choir roof remain to be built, there is good hope that this fine building can now be completed.

New York (St. Patrick's Cathedral). The most famous Roman Catholic cathedral in the USA is St. Patrick's, once standing out prominently on Fifth Avenue but now surrounded on all sides by taller buildings and overshadowed by the towers of the Rockefeller Centre. It is the work of a young American architect, James Renwick, who was an admirer of mediaeval Gothic and, using modern methods (the frame is of iron girders), erected an impressive church with twin octagonal western towers and spires rising to 100.5 m (330 ft) with a fine rose-window between them. Built on the hard rock of which Manhattan is formed, granite was used for the foundations and the base of the walls which are faced with marble.

Washington. St. Peter and St. Paul Cathedral at Washington is, like St. John the Divine at New York, unfinished. Originally designed by the eminent English Victorian architect, G.F. Bodley, work was begun in 1907. Not having to contend with tower blocks, it dominates the skyline and is a notable building standing on the top of Mount St. Albans, the highest point in the city and set in spacious and attractive gardens. English in appearance with its central tower a loftier and larger edition of the central tower of Wells, although apsed, it contrasts with the French-inspired New York cathedrals. It is built of Indiana limestone.

Many different groups worship in it, Russian Orthodox, Jewish and several other congregations as well as Episcopalians and there are many reminders of the great figures of American history, especially the kneeling figure of Abraham Lincoln, a fine statue of George Washington, and American heroes in the stained glass windows.

Glossary

AMBO: An early Christian raised reading-desk or pulpit.

AMBULATORY: Semicircular or polygonal aisle.

APSE: Semicircular or polygonal termination to church or chapel.

BALDACCHINO: Canopy supported on columns.

BALUSTER: Small pillar usually circular and swelling in the middle or towards the base.

CHANTRY CHAPEL: A small chapel endowed for the saying of Masses for the soul of the donor.

CHAPTER HOUSE: The place of assembly for dean and canons.

CHEVET: East end comprising apse, ambulatory and radiating chapels.

CLERESTORY: Upper storey of nave, choir and transepts, pierced by row of windows set above roofs of the aisles.

CONFESSIO: Opening for venerating relics or shrine placed in a crypt.

CORBEL: Stone bracket.

CORO: Enclosed choir in nave.

CORONA: Crown of tower or apsed eastern termination.

FOUR-CENTRED ARCH: Pointed arch in which voussoirs spring from two pairs of centres.

ICONOSTASIS: Screen of icons separating sanctuary from rest of church.

MISERICORD: Bracket on the underside of hinged wooden seat in choir stall, often enriched with lively carvings.

NARTHEX: Enclosed portico or vestibule at western end of church between entrance and nave.

RETABLE: Picture or piece of carving, standing behind and attached to altar.

REREDOS: Wall or screen behind altar, usually ornamented.

ROOD-SCREEN: Stone or wooden screen below rood, separating chancel from nave.

SEDILIA: Recessed stone seats in chancel for priest and assistants.

TRACERY: (a) *Plate*. Early form in which shapes are cut from solid stone of window head.

        (b) *Bar*. Curved and intersecting slender shafts which follow lines of mullions.

        (c) *Geometrical*. mainly circles, often foiled.

(d) *Reticulated*. Ogee shapes producing net-like pattern.

(e) *Flowing*. Later Decorated forms in which circular and ogee-shapes are eliminated.

(f) *Perpendicular*. Rectilinear form in which vertical bars (mullions) carry up into head of window and cross-bars or transoms are introduced.

TRIFORIUM: Arcaded wall passage or area of blank arcading above main arcade.

TRUMEAU: Pillar dividing a doorway.

VAULT: Arched roof of stone.

(a) *Barrel*. Simple, rounded, like a tunnel.

(b) *Groined*. When two barrel vaults intersect.

(c) *Rib*. With diagonal ribs projecting along the groin.

(d) *Tierceron*. With extra ribs springing from same point as principal ribs but which meet obliquely.

(e) *Lierne*. Incorporating decorative short, subsidiary ribs (liernes).

(f) *Fan*. In which the length and curvature of the ribs, which spring from the same point, are similar.

VOUSSOIR: Wedge-shaped stone of an arch.

Bibliography

I have been much helped by guide-books: Baedeker, Fodor, Michelin, Pitkin, Ward Lock and the Blue Guides. The following deal more specifically with architecture:

Aubert, Marcel, *Gothic Cathedrals of France and their Treasures* (Nicholas Kaye, 1959).

Bumpus, T. Francis, *The Cathedrals and Churches of Belgium* (T. Werner Laurie).

Clifton-Taylor, Alec, *The Cathedrals of England* (Thames & Hudson, 1967).

Franklin, J. W., *The Cathedrals of Italy* (B. T. Batsford, 1958).

Grant, Neil, *Cathedrals* (Franklin Watts).

Hamilton, George Heard, *The Art and Architecture of Russia. In: The Pelican History of Art*. Edited by: Nikolaus Pevsner and Judy Nairn. (Penguin Books, 1954 [Second edition, 1975].)

Harvey, John, *The Cathedrals of Spain* (B. T. Batsford, 1957).

Henderson, Helen, *Cathedrals of France* (Methuen & Co., 1929).

Houghton, Leighton, *A Guide to the British Cathedrals* (John Baker, 1973).

Hürlimann, M. (Photographs) and Bony, Jean (Introduction), *French Cathedrals* (Thames & Hudson, 1951 [New edition 1961]).

Little, Bryan, *English Cathedrals in Colour* (B. T. Batsford, 1972).

National Belgian Tourist Office, *Cathedrals and Town Halls 1975. European Architectural Heritage Year*.

New, Anthony, S. B., *The Observer's Book of Cathedrals* (Frederick Warne & Co., 1972).

Norwich, John Julius (Editor), *Great Architecture of the World* (Mitchell Beazley, 1975).

Schmidt-Glassner, Helga (Photographs) and Baum, Julius (Introduction), *German Cathedrals* (Thames & Hudson, 1956).

Van Simson, Otto, *The Gothic Cathedral* (Pantheon Books, 1956). Bollingen Services XLVIII.

Wolgensinger, Michael (Photographs), *Cathedrals of Europe* (Elsevier-Phaidon. Published in Great Britain, 1976).

Index

The figures in bold refer to colour plates. Those in italics refer to the page numbers of black and white illustrations. Other figures refer to text pages.